GROWING UP
CATHOLIC

GROWING UP CATHOLIC

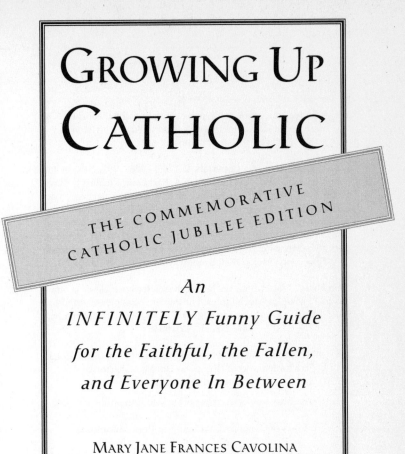

THE COMMEMORATIVE
CATHOLIC JUBILEE EDITION

An
INFINITELY Funny Guide
for the Faithful, the Fallen,
and Everyone In Between

MARY JANE FRANCES CAVOLINA
JEFFREY ALLEN JOSEPH STONE
MAUREEN ANNE TERESA KELLY
RICHARD GLEN MICHAEL DAVIS

Illustrations by Bob Kiley
and Bob Jones

Broadway Books   New York

BROADWAY

An earlier edition of this book was originally published in 1985 by
Main Street Books, an imprint of Doubleday, a division of
Random House, Inc.

Broadway Books titles may be purchased for business or promo-
tional use or for special sales. For information, please write to:
Special Markets Department, Random House, Inc., 1540 Broadway,
New York, NY 10036.

BROADWAY BOOKS and its logo, a letter B bisected on the diagonal,
are trademarks of Broadway Books, a division of
Random House, Inc.

First Broadway Books trade paperback edition published 2000.

Library of Congress Cataloging-in-Publication Data

Growing up Catholic: an infinitely funny guide for the faithful, the
fallen, and everyone in between/Mary Jane Frances Cavolina . . .
[et al.]; illustrations by Bob Kiley and Bob Jones.—Commemorative
Catholic jubilee ed.
        p. cm.
    1. Catholic Church—Humor.   2. Catholic Church—
United States—History—20th century—Humor.   3. United
States—Church history—20th century—Humor.   4. Catholic wit
and humor.   5. American wit and humor.
        I. Cavolina, Mary Jane Frances, 1954–
                BX1755.G76 2000
        282′.73′0207—dc21   00-023708

ISBN 0-7679-0597-0

00   01   02   03   04   10   9   8   7   6   5   4   3   2   1

With love to
Frank and Shirley Cavolina;
Anne and Norman Stone, Nora Flaherty, and James Morris;
Ethan, Hannah, and Abigail;
and Donald and Rita Davis

And to the parish priests who guided us;
the nuns, brothers, and lay teachers who taught us
to read and to write, but mostly to respect and be respected;
to the Church that taught us that loving concern
for those around us is our highest achievement:
your examples of love, selflessness,
and dedication will always guide us.

ACKNOWLEDGMENTS

To Margaret Anne Anne Ruley, who was there "in the beginning"; her divine inspiration helped set us on our way; and to Michele Farinet, whose sense of humor and enthusiasm added immeasurably.

To Elaine Markson, Raymond Bongiovanni, and Geri Thoma for their early faith in our idea and all their hard work to make a book happen; to our editor, Loretta Anne Anne Barrett, whose unfailing encouragement, empathy, and guidance in the fine points of Catholic doctrine provided the best possible creative atmosphere in which to work.

To Laura Worsham, who took many of the original photographs.

To our friends, especially Bob Asahina, Matthew Bunson, and David Earle.

And to our families, who contributed in so many ways, whether they knew it or not—Ellen, Josh, Lisa, Robbie, Larry, Lorraine, Michael and Joan Cavolina, Grandma, and my sweet little Rocky; Greg, Ted and Sue Stone, and Liz and Larry Strach; and Anne, Kevin, Claire, Patrick, and Vincent Kelly.

And to the gang at Broadway Books: Gerry Howard, Charlie Conrad, Becky Cole, Catherine Pollock, Toby Cox, Debbie Stier, and Nancy Clare Morgan, for still believing.

CONTENTS

V
CATHOLICS AT LARGE

VI
INFINITE THY VAST DOMAIN

INTRODUCTION
to the Jubilee Edition

Every Catholic, whether devout, practicing, grudgingly observant, lapsed or excommunicated, shares with millions of other Catholics the indelible marks of his or her upbringing. In Philadelphia and Omaha, at Immaculate Heart and St. Pius X, the teaching nuns wielded their rulers with the same ruthless efficiency, the same Hail Marys were said as penance for lying to your parents and you had to get to Mass before the Gospel or you wouldn't "fulfill the obligation" and you'd end up in a state of mortal sin.

But what does it mean to be a Catholic these days? Many of the old rules and regulations apply, but much has changed. Confession, conducted en masse, is known as the Sacrament of Reconciliation; the Bishop is leading the statewide antinuclear movement; St. Christopher was demoted; and Holy Days of Obligation were almost made optional.

It is not only Catholics themselves who appear to have a renewed interest in their religious identity and heritage. The prominence of priests, nuns and the Church in popular culture, and of the Pope in the news, suggests that Catholicism is fascinating both to those raised in the Church and to those who wondered why their Catholic friends had to eat fish sticks on Friday until 1965. Catholicism seems to have acquired a mystique, even a certain cachet.

This book reflects the authors' own personal perceptions of Roman Catholicism over the past three decades, as we grew up and matured. The experiences of Catholics born after the mid-1960s will be very different from ours. Catholics older than we will undoubtedly have their own peculiar memories and attitudes, in addition to the ones we recall here.

Still, much of the Catholic heritage is a constant, or nearly so. No matter what your age or where you come from, you'll see in this book the major elements of our shared memories and experience—our dress, our speech, our posture, our imaginations, our guardian angels, our rituals, our handwriting, our values, our uniforms—which touch the farthest corners of our lives and constitute our shared cultural, social and religious heritage.

For us, this book is a looking back and a partial summing up, an assessment of the effect of Catholicism on our memories, our sense of humor, and, yes, our souls. We hope that in reading it other Catholics will also see themselves, and that our non-Catholic friends will understand our jokes better. Catholics will know not to look for an imprimatur.

We wrote those words as the Introduction to the original edition of *Growing Up Catholic* in February of 1985. Fifteen years later, we look back on the Church of our childhood from a greater distance, but with no less affection and laughter. When we were in grammar school, we computed how old we'd be in the year 2000, never quite believing that it would arrive, or that we would ever be that old. And yet it has come—not just as the big rollover on the celestial odometer, but as a major milestone in the history of the Catholic Church, the two thousandth anniversary of the birth of Jesus Christ. (After all, let's not forget where this whole millennium thing came from anyway!)

In the world we grew up in, you knew who was Catholic and who wasn't. Catholics did things that other people didn't do; they were conspicuous. They ate fish on Fridays, wore Miraculous Medals around their necks, blessed themselves when a fire engine went by, went to Mass every Sunday, come hell or high water (literally), and said the name of their parish when they told people where they came from. Nowadays it's hard to tell if the guy in the next cubicle is Catholic or not, except on Ash Wednesday. These days it seems we must carry our Catholicism inside us, and so it is more important than ever to remember who we are, and to reinforce the communion our shared history brings.

Since 1985, a whole new generation of Catholics has grown up without ever hearing a word of Latin at Mass, or seeing a wimple except in a movie or on Halloween. Yet despite appearances, the core of our Catholicism is fundamentally unchanged. Catholics still believe that each human being is ultimately responsible for his or her actions, and that those actions have real, even eternal, consequences. The old Church favored the term "examination of conscience." Modern Catholics might not use those words exactly, but the basic Catholic reflex is the same. We are forever asking ourselves: Was what I did right or wrong? Good or evil? How can I do better next time?

We wrote *Growing Up Catholic* in the belief, developed in our conversations with one another, that the funny and sublime side of day-to-day Catholic life was the same for everyone. Gratifyingly, the book was warmly received. We were relieved to hear that priests quoted it in their sermons. At least one Cardinal mentioned it in church, and it is our fondest hope that maybe even the Pope has, well, at least heard of it. Most of all, we were happy to find that Regular Catholics like us enjoyed reading our book, and that it helped to stir up their own memories.

This Jubilee edition includes the full text of the original edition of *Growing Up Catholic,* and highlights of its two sequels, *More Growing Up Catholic* and *Still Catholic After All These Years,* as well as new material. Jubilee 2000, declared by Pope John Paul II, is an extraordinary moment, a time for looking back and rejoicing. So look back and rejoice.

Who made us?
God made us.

Who is God?
God is the Supreme Being, infinitely perfect, who made all things and keeps them in existence.

Why did God make us?
God made us to show forth His goodness and to share with us His everlasting happiness in heaven.

What must we do to gain the happiness of heaven?
To gain the happiness of heaven we must know, love, and serve God in this world.

From whom do we learn to know, love, and serve God?
We learn to know, love, and serve God from Jesus Christ, the Son of God, who teaches us through the Catholic Church.

1

I Am a Catholic. In Case of Accident, Please Call a Priest.

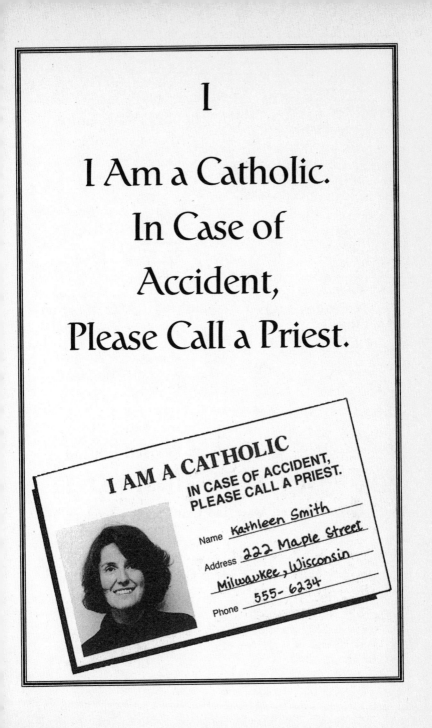

Rt. Rev. Msgr. Michael A. McGuire

Pastor of the Church
of St. Frances of Rome
Bronx, New York

- Illustrated
- Study Helps
- Word Meanings
- Phoneticized Vocabulary

New Revised Edition

BALTIMORE CATECHISM NO. 2

With Special Prayer, Mass and Confirmation Sections

BENZIGER BROTHERS, INC.
Printers to the Holy Apostolic See
New York   Boston   Cincinnati   Chicago   San Francisco

THE BALTIMORE CATECHISM:
Basic Training for Young Catholics

THE PROBLEM

How to educate young Catholic minds in the teachings of the Church and give them a solid grounding—a rock, so to speak—on which to build their faith.

THE SOLUTION

Design a book that puts together the most complex theological issues, the greatest mysteries of the faith and the ways and means of performing Catholic ritual, and make it understandable to a seven-year-old, even though most of the greatest thinkers of the ages haven't quite figured it all out. Call it the *Baltimore Catechism* and make everyone memorize it.

Why is this book called the *Baltimore Catechism*?

This book is called the *Baltimore Catechism* because the catechism written in it was discussed in Baltimore.

Where can you get a copy of the *Baltimore Catechism*?

You can get one free while attending a Catholic grade school, or you can buy a copy in a religious articles store.

How many editions has the *Baltimore Catechism* had?

The *Baltimore Catechism* has had many editions, all of which are right and true.

How can you use the *Baltimore Catechism*?

You can and should use the *Baltimore Catechism* to lead a good Catholic life and attain Heaven.

What will happen if you do not use what you learn in the *Baltimore Catechism?*
    You will go to Hell.

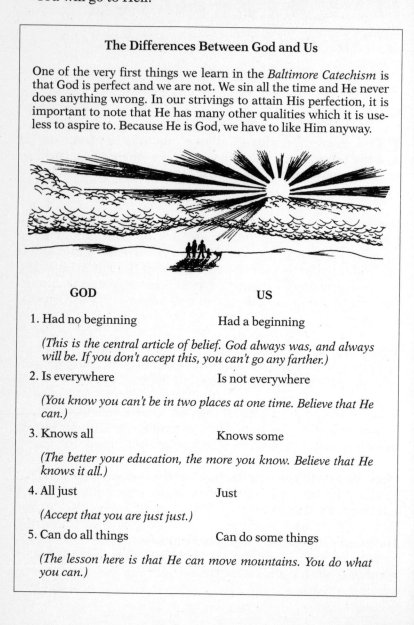

The Differences Between God and Us

One of the very first things we learn in the *Baltimore Catechism* is that God is perfect and we are not. We sin all the time and He never does anything wrong. In our strivings to attain His perfection, it is important to note that He has many other qualities which it is useless to aspire to. Because He is God, we have to like Him anyway.

GOD	US
1. Had no beginning	Had a beginning

(This is the central article of belief. God always was, and always will be. If you don't accept this, you can't go any farther.)

2. Is everywhere	Is not everywhere

(You know you can't be in two places at one time. Believe that He can.)

3. Knows all	Knows some

(The better your education, the more you know. Believe that He knows it all.)

4. All just	Just

(Accept that you are just just.)

5. Can do all things	Can do some things

(The lesson here is that He can move mountains. You do what you can.)

THROUGH MY FAULT, THROUGH MY FAULT:
The Problem of Sin

Catholicism has more rules and regulations which enable you to sin than any other religion. Our preoccupation with sin is the central difference between us and everyone else. We are consumed with it; and why not? These blemishes on our souls can keep us out of Heaven, put us in Purgatory for aeons, or, God forbid, hurl us into Hell for ever and ever amen. Catholic life, then, is filled with high drama; moral tension is injected into every act.

To begin with, we are born with Original Sin—like factory seconds, slightly imperfect. Baptism wipes Original Sin away, and from then on it's up to us to get our own sins and to get rid of them.

There are two kinds of sin, mortal (the more serious kind) and venial. Committing a mortal sin means knowing that what you are about to do, think, want or say is really bad, but doing, thinking, wanting or saying it anyway.

Most of the things we do wrong fall into the somewhat less offensive category of venial sin. Committing a venial sin means doing something that is not really so bad, or doing something really bad that you don't *think* is really bad or that your heart isn't really into doing. If your little brother is being a pest and you tell him to drop dead, you've committed a venial sin. If you shoot him dead, you've committed a mortal sin.

While on the surface the differences between mortal and venial sin seem obvious, don't be fooled. There is more to this than meets the eye. What is "really bad" and what isn't? And more to the point, *who decides*?

Let's take a routine situation and note all the possible pitfalls:

You are at a baseball game on a Friday night. You are not supposed to eat meat on Friday. You want a hot dog.

Now, just considering eating meat on Friday is a venial sin;

wanting to is another one. You have not moved in your seat and you have already sinned twice. What if you actually ate one? Aside from the risk of choking on forbidden food and receiving your temporal punishment on the spot, have you committed a mortal sin or a venial sin? Well, if you think it's mortal, it may be mortal; and if you think it's venial, it still may be mortal. After much thought, you decide it's venial. You call the hot-dog vendor, you take the money out of your pocket and you buy a hot dog. This is clearly an act of free will. You figure you can go to Confession on Saturday. But wait! Does a venial sin become mortal when you commit it deliberately? That's a chance you take. What if you've forgotten

it's Friday? In that case, eating the hot dog may not be a sin, but forgetting it's Friday is. What if you remember it's Friday halfway through the hot dog? Is it a venial sin to finish it? If you throw it away, is wasting food a sin? Within five minutes you have committed enough sins to land you in Purgatory for a million years. The simplest course is just not to take any chances. *Avoid the near occasion of sin.* Stay out of the ball park on Fridays.

Being a Catholic means fighting a lifelong struggle to avoid sin, mortal or venial. While you don't want to go to Hell, you definitely don't want to rot in Purgatory either. Play it safe. Think about every thought, word, action, desire and omission. Figure that everything you want to do is a sin.

BLESS ME, FATHER

As was to be expected, sometime between last Saturday's confession and this Saturday, you've sinned. You know because you feel guilty. It is time to go to Confession once again. Even though you won't go to Hell if you die with only venial sins on your soul, and you don't think you did anything *that* bad, it's not worth the risk. Sins are easy to get, but they're just as easy to get rid of.

EXAMINATION OF CONSCIENCE

It is a good idea to examine your conscience before going to Confession. Even if you think the only thing you did wrong this week was to cheat on Mrs. Rostik's science test, confessing only one sin will make the priest doubt your sincerity and will sound like you think you're some kind of saint. Also, as insurance against those sins you may have forgotten or not realized you committed, it can't hurt to throw in a few extra. If you really think about it, you will come up with more.

The Near Occasion of Sin: How Near Is Near?

The omnipresent Near Occasion can take the form of a person, place or thing.

Hanging around with the wrong crowd, for example, exposes you to Bad Companions. A Bad Companion is a "friend" who encourages you to go to the local pool to see girls in their bathing suits, or who suggests that you see a movie more risqué than *Lassie Come Home*.

The Near Occasion might also be your grandparents' home. If, for example, your grandfather has a cache of *Playboy* magazines, it would be wise not to visit, even if this means missing Thanksgiving dinner. If you explain properly, your mother will understand.

It is things, however, that tend to be the most difficult Near Occasions to shun—movies, dirty magazines, cigarettes, alcohol, etc. Since it is always better to be safe than a sinner, the best way to avoid the things that could lead to sin is to find a place where no temptations exist. You might try a perfectly white room that contains no offending objects, secured with a deadbolt lock to keep out Bad Companions. If you stay in this room a significant part of your life, you will generally be able to avoid the Near Occasion.

Sin/Indulgence Balance Sheet

Although we are taught that indulgences—certain prayers, ejaculations and actions—will help take away some of the punishment for our sins, they do not really make a dent in your time in Purgatory. One week's indulgences do not, as you can see, mark a significant change in the punishment accrued for one day's sins.

SINS (1 day)		INDULGENCES (1 week)	
Lied to your mother	650,000 years	Said Grace before dinner every day	21 years
Cheated on test	825,000 years	Said Mother of	
Stole candy bar	257,890 years	Mercy, Pray for	
Stuck tongue out at Sister	1,160,000 years	Us 315 times on the way in to class on Thurs-	
Spilled milk on uniform	456,000 years	day	259 years
	_____	Served Mass on	
	3,348,890 years	Tuesday and	
	− 286 years	Sunday	6 years
	_____		_____
	3,348,604 years		286 years

Although you can examine your conscience in advance, it is better to do it in church before getting in line for Confession. The holy surroundings will make every little thing you did that week seem far worse than they really were, and will assure you of having a good list of things to tell the priest.

When you enter the church, bless yourself with somewhat more piety than usual. You are about to receive a sacrament. Select an empty pew, genuflect solemnly and enter. Go directly into the kneeling position and bury your face in your hands for maximum concentration. Think hard about the past week.

Did you tell your mother to shut up? Yes. Did you hit your dog? Yes. Were you mean to your brothers and sisters? Yes. Did you make a face at Sister behind her back? Yes. If you're really stumped for sins, remember that omission is also a sin. Did you share your lunch with Nicholas when he forgot his? No. Did you help Mrs. Thomas carry her packages home from the store when she passed you playing baseball? No. There is a whole range of "I didn'ts" to choose from. The priest will know that you are very holy for even thinking of these things.

Once you know exactly what you have and haven't done, memorize the list so you won't forget in the confessional. Now go and get in line. Be sure to go to the priest who gives the most lenient penances—look for the longest line.

CONFESSION

There are four or five people ahead of you on your side of the confessional. There are four or five on the other side, too. Use this valuable waiting time to say the Bless Me, Father prayer over and over again to be sure you don't forget *that* in the confessional either. If you do the priest will think you haven't been to Confession in a very long time. Once you're sure you know it, start saying ejaculations (My Jesus, Mercy, for example) and offer them up for the souls in Purgatory. Do not think about why the man who just went into the confessional is taking so long.

It is finally your turn. The person coming out will hold the curtain for you. Kneel

down. Wait while the priest hears the confession of the person on the other side. Do not listen. If the other person is talking louder than she should, pray to distract yourself. When he's ready for you, Father will open the grate in front of your face. Rattle it all off without a hitch. Do not confess adultery. It does not mean "being dirty." The priest will then give you your penance. If you have to say a

True Confessions

From the most confessed to the least confessed real and imagined sins:

1. Talking back to your parents
2. Disobeying your parents
3. Not doing your chores
4. Fighting with your brother(s)/sister(s)/schoolmate(s)
5. Telling a lie
6. Swearing
7. Impure thoughts
8. Impure acts (boys)
9. Stealing
10. Being unkind
11. Missing Mass on a Holy Day of Obligation
12. Missing Mass on a Sunday
13. Participating in a Protestant service
14. Impure acts (girls)
15. Murder

lot of prayers, he thought you did some bad things.

Leave the confessional, remembering to hold the curtain for the next person in line. Go straight to the altar rail, kneel down, bless yourself and say your penance. In the spiritual intensity of the moment, you may decide to light a candle with the quarter you've saved for candy. Try not to be sorry later. When you leave the church ask your friends, "Whadja get?" and compare penances.

You are free of your sins. Now you definitely will not go to Hell if you die before committing your next sin—a good incentive for keeping the slate clean. You should go to Confession anytime you want to receive, and anytime you are in danger of sudden death, like before getting on an airplane. If you have not thought of this and you know you are going to die in a state of mortal sin, say a "perfect" Act of Contrition and hope that what's perfect to you is perfect to Him.

O MY GOD, I AM HARDLY SORRY

Prayer is an integral part of the life of a Catholic. A way of talking to God, prayer has as many options as does talking to anyone else whom you know.

WHOM WE PRAY TO

1. God (to praise Him or to ask a favor)
2. Mary (to ask her to intercede with her Son on our behalf)
3. Saints (the religious form of going to a specialist when you have an ailment, because patron saints have great sway in their particular quarter. If something is lost, cut the red tape and go straight to St. Anthony.)

WHERE WE PRAY

1. At home
2. At school
3. In church
4. At work
5. On the bus
6. Anywhere else we want to

HOW WE PRAY

1. Silently
2. Out loud
3. Alone
4. In groups
5. Formally (using the prayers we memorized in school)
6. Informally (making up prayers as we go along)
7. Kneeling
8. Sitting
9. Standing
10. Lying down (particularly when you are dangerously ill)

WHY WE PRAY

1. We are in trouble
2. We are frightened
3. For a good intention
4. To ask for the well-being of our family and friends
5. To offer up for the souls in Purgatory
6. To say thank you
7. To say please

WHEN WE PRAY

1. When we get up in the morning
2. When we go to bed at night
3. Before we eat
4. After we eat
5. Before class begins
6. Before a test
7. At Mass
8. After Confession
9. Before participating in a sporting event (swimmers have the advantage of being able to dip their fingers in the pool before blessing themselves)

WHEN WE PRAY QUICKLY

1. To get our penance over with
2. To get our Rosary over with
3. To get through a prayer before we forget the words (the presence of a nun with a ruler leads to record-breaking times)
4. To gather indulgences quickly (an ejaculation that takes 300 days off Purgatory can easily be said 500 times between classes, knocking almost 410 years off, counting leap years)

Prayer: A Pop Quiz

As a result of the terror struck into the hearts of schoolchildren by nuns who commanded rote memorization of prayers under pain of humiliation at the business end of a ruler, any Catholic who is given the first few words of a prayer can rattle out the rest of it, often in both English and Latin. Proof of the efficacy of their teaching methods is the fact that this holds true even if the prayer in question has not been said in twenty years. But start a Catholic off in the middle of a prayer and the situation is hopeless.

Do you know the names of the prayers from which these phrases come?

1. *"I believe these and all the truths which the Holy Catholic Church teaches, because Thou hast revealed them."*
2. *"Pray for us sinners, now and at the hour of our death."*
3. *"I detest all my sins, because of Thy just punishment, but most of all be-*

cause they offend Thee, my God, who art all-good and deserving of all my love."
4. *"I believe in the Holy Ghost, the Holy Catholic Church, the communion of saints, the forgiveness of sins, the resurrection of the body, and life everlasting."*
5. *"I hope to obtain pardon of my sins, the help of Thy grace, and life everlasting, through the merits of Jesus Christ, my Lord and Redeemer."*
6. *"O my God, I love thee above all things, with my whole heart and soul, because Thou art all-good and worthy of all love."*
7. *"Forgive us our trespasses as we forgive those who trespass against us."*
8. *"To thee do we cry, poor banished children of Eve; to thee do we send up our sighs, mourning and weeping in this vale of tears."*

Answers: 1. Act of Faith 2. Hail Mary 3. Act of Contrition 4. Apostles' Creed 5. Act of Hope 6. Act of Love 7. The Lord's Prayer 8. Hail, Holy Queen

Patron Saints Matching Column

1. Nicholas
2. Hilary
3. Timothy and Titus
4. Herbert
5. Mark
6. James
7. Dymphna
8. Harvey
9. Martha
10. Lydia
11. Clare
12. Bartholomew
13. Fiacre
14. Bruno
15. Teresa of Avila
16. Luke

A. Cooks
B. Notaries
C. Headache sufferers
D. Invoked against sore eyes
E. Bakers and pawnbrokers
F. Mentally Ill
G. Doctors and painters
H. Plasterers
I. Invoked against stomach
   disorders
J. Gardeners and cab drivers
K. Invoked against snake bites
L. Invoked against eye sores
M. Hatmakers
N. Those possessed
O. Invoked in time of drought
P. Dyers

Answers:

1. E.; 2. K.; 3. I.; 4. O.; 5. B.; 6.
M.; 7. F.; 8. L.; 9. A.; 10. P.; 11.
D.; 12. H.; 13. J.; 14. N.; 15. C.;
16. G.

THE FAMILY THAT PRAYS TOGETHER

One of the most important times we pray is at home with our family. Prayers recited from our earliest years with our parents and brothers and sisters were not merely soothing bedtime rituals. Although we later learn the fine points of our religion in school, it is in the home that we are taught the fundamentals, as much by deed as by word.

Catholic parents are obligated to train their offspring in the faith and indeed promise—in writing—to do so when they marry. What's more, they're obligated to have us in the first

Beyond the Vows

The lovely nuptial Mass has ended, the last crumb of wedding cake devoured and the final good-byes said. At last, the newly married couple hops into their gaily decorated car to drive off into the sunset.

During their pre-Cana sessions, the newlyweds had been instructed in the one method of birth control sanctioned by the Catholic Church— the rhythm method. Its success rate can be measured by the average number of children in Catholic families. Nonetheless, the intricate graphs are fun to chart and, after all, children are a blessing from God.

A Catholic Woman's Rhythm Diary

Week 1
Safe for a few days.

Week 2
Sat. nite K of C dinner dance. Gerry feeling especially romantic. Getting risky. Could be trouble.

Week 3
Temperature up a bit but could be touch of flu. Fingers crossed.

Week 4
Temp. still up. This hasn't happened in a while. Please God.

Week 5
Ten Rosaries offered up to St. Jude. [Patron saint of lost causes.] *Long visit with Mary Ellen.* [Her sister.] *Schedule appointment with Dr. O'Malley.*

Week 6
Jesus, Mary and Joseph!

Week 7
Get Gerry to pick up bassinet from Mom.

place, because the Church says the only reason to have you-know-what is procreation. And so it's children, and lots of them, that set Catholic families apart from all the rest.

Acceptable Catholic Swears—

often used by Catholic couples after an unsuccessful bout with the rhythm method

Glory be
Jesus, Mary and Joseph
Heavens!
Saints be praised (favorite of nuns)
Mercy
Dio mio or Mon Dieu

TAKE ME TO THE RIVER

The first obligation of Catholic parent to child is getting the little one baptized. Baptism wipes out Original Sin and should be performed as soon after birth as possible. This is because formerly, unbaptized infants went to Limbo along with heathens and other non-Catholics who did not know they had Original Sin and so didn't do anything about it. (Some Catholic nurses apparently did. It was rumored that they would baptize every child under their care, irrespective of religion. The Church made it easy for emergency Baptisms to be performed: anyone could do it, and all you needed was tap water.)

Original Sin does not mean you have invented a new crime. It is every human being's inheritance from Adam and Eve. Some people think that Adam and Eve's sin was eating the forbidden fruit;

others believe it involved sex. Certainly anything combining fruit and sex is a kinky exercise and frowned upon by the Church.

It is only in extraordinary cases that the newborn infant is able to respond for himself during the actual Baptism ceremony, so it is up to his godparents to renounce Satan for him and pledge that he will live according to the teachings of Christ and the Church. Since it will be their duty to raise the child in the faith if anything should happen to the parents, the godparents should be Good Catholics. Wealth and influence are also nice, since the godparent remains a lifelong resource.

Arrangements for the Baptism are made several weeks in advance. On the appointed day, baby is swaddled in a christening dress—that's dress, regardless of sex. Not unlike a tiny wedding dress, this is a garment made up of layers and layers of white lacy fabric, and is often handed down from generation to generation. However, it will probably die of overuse rather than old age, owing to the considerable size of most Catholic families.

Parents, godparents, family members and a few close friends all put on their best Sunday best and meet at the church—usually on a Saturday. They greet the priest and proceed to the baptismal font. At the ceremony's climax, the priest pours a little water on the child's head, anoints it with holy oil and puts a bit of salt on the child's tongue. In some cases a small part of the child's body—say, a toe—is inserted into the water in the font. This is known as Baptism by immersion. Watch the heirloom christening dress! Whatever the variation, the ritual symbolizes spiritual birth. After the ceremony, everyone goes back to the baby's parents' house and eats too much.

STICKS AND STONES

As far as the Church is concerned, Baptism is when a child is officially named. Exceptionally devout parents might consider calling their child Baby Doe until the baptismal certificate is signed and sealed. Generally, however, by the time of Baptism the child has had a name for several weeks, the civil authorities have been informed of it and it has been inscribed on the birth certificate. This time sequence can cause problems:

Appropriate Names for Catholic Children

Traditional: Any saint's name, particularly Mary, Theresa, Margaret, Anne and Elizabeth for girls; Joseph, John, Thomas, James and Michael for boys.
Less Traditional: Trendy first name followed by saint's name; that is, Jennifer Margaret, Scott Francis, Justin Joseph.

Totally Unacceptable Names for Catholic Children

Gidget
Isaac
Sunshine
Jesus (surprising, but no, unless combined with Spanish surname)
Cheryl (Contrary to popular belief, there was never a St. Cheryl.)
Gay
Todd
Trevor
Chet
Moon Unit
Tiffany
Jo, as a middle name for girls: Sally Jo, Billie Jo, Betty Jo. (Exception: Mary Jo. Mary in any name position cancels out any non-Catholic influence.)
Bob, as a middle name for boys: Jim Bob, Joe Bob, Iver Bob (no exceptions whatsoever)

---

the proud parents may show up at the christening armed with the baby and a name the priest does no approve. A Catholic child is expected to bear a saint's name or a derivation thereof. The idea is that the chosen saint will serve as a spiritual role model and protector. A Church that calls many parishes Holy Name takes such things seriously.

"But 'Wendy' is derived from 'Gwendolyn.' That's a saint's name," the parents protest. " 'Wendy' is a name created by Sir James Barrie in the early part of this century when he wrote *Peter Pan,*" the priest replies. "Damned Jesuit sophistry," the parents think. "But 'Tammy' is a derivative of 'Thomasina.' That's a derivative of 'Thomas.' That's a saint's name." "Wrong, simply wrong," Father says emphatically.

Of course, no one knows where this name came from, but parents who would give it to a child obviously don't care where they came from either. "But 'Tab'—" the parents begin. "—Is a soft drink," Father finishes, and you should accept his judgment on aesthetic grounds if not religious ones.

You can always fix everything up by following an

unorthodox first name with a saint's name in the middle. Or you can try the very subtle and probably theologically sound argument that though there may be no canonized saint by the name you have chosen, there is sure to be a worthy but un-canonized one. Most likely this will not cut the mustard at St. Rocco's.

After you have agonized over a choice acceptable to you, your spouse *and* your priest, remember that only you and the grade school nuns will ever call your child by his baptismal name.

11

Good
Morning,
Sister

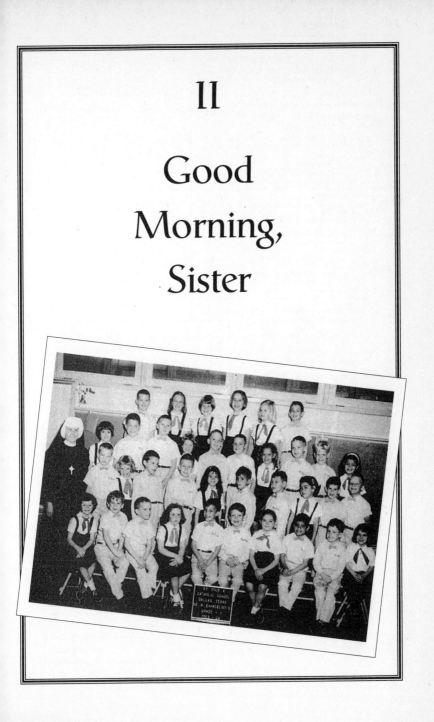

CATHOLIC ELEMENTARY SCHOOLS
DIOCESE OF BROOKLYN

Name of School _St. Luke's_

Grade School Hours: 9-12 : 1-3   Kg. School Hours _____

Dear Parent or Guardian:

The school needs your cooperation in aiding the growth of your child in religious habits, scholarship, health and character.

The home must assume the responsibility with the Church and the School in stressing piety by making the basic virtues directly appear in the daily conduct of your child. The real meaning of life can be better grasped by your child only when the home supplies the moral guidance by example.

The principal and the teacher will gladly help you in your God given task.

FIRST TERM ENDING _____

Principal _____

Teacher _____

SIGNATURE OF PARENT OR GUARDIAN

Mid-Term: _____

Final: _____

SECOND TERM ENDING _June_

Principal _S. M. Benedicta_

Teacher _S. Jean Patrice_

SIGNATURE OF PARENT OR GUARDIAN

Mid-Term _Mrs John D. Gregorio_

Final _____

REPORT CARD
Kindergarten — Grade 2B

Name _Louise DiGregorio_

Res. _2-0-49-10 St._

Grade _____   Grade _A_

STANDING—A-EXCELLENT; B-GOOD; C-FAIR; D-POOR

FIRST TERM		SUBJECTS	SECOND TERM	
MID-TERM	TERM		MID-TERM	TERM
		RELIGION	80	90
		ENGLISH	75	85
		READING READINESS	78	72
		WRITING	85	87
		SPELLING (2ND YEAR)	65	82
		ARITHMETIC	76	84
		ART	a	a
		MUSIC	a	a
		HEALTH EDUCATION	a	a
		Average	78.2	83.3
		RELIGIOUS	B+	a
		WORK	B	B+
		PERSONAL	a	a
		CLEANLINESS	a	a
		SOCIAL	a	a
		NEATNESS	B+	B+
		PROPERTY CARE	a	a
		SELF CONTROL	a	a
		CONDUCT	a	a
		EFFORT	B	B
		MASS ABSENCES		
		COMMUNIONS REC'D		
		DAYS PRESENT	40	42
		DAYS ABSENT	3	11
		TIMES LATE		

PROMOTED: _____   PROMOTED: _yes_

LESSON 3
SISTER SAYS:
Nine to Three in Holier Than Thou

TO HELP YOU UNDERSTAND THIS LESSON

In parochial grammar schools, the three *R*'s take a backseat to the alphabet soup of virtues the nuns drill into their sacred charges. Catholic schoolchildren's lives are demanding ones, what with being honest, brave, charitable, obedient, respectful, and clean in thought, word and deed. They have more important things on their minds than the multiplication tables, like worrying about the state of their immortal souls, which would be jeopardized by not hanging up their uniforms or not keeping their notebooks neat and clean. While their non-Catholic friends are shooting spitwads, passing notes, making fun of their teachers, and generally having a good time, they are slogging through Boot Camp on the way to becoming soldiers of Christ. The nuns are there to help them out, and they mean business. Parochial schoolchildren are disciplined, uniformed, lined up, paraded, processioned, marched and drilled by nuns who wield their rulers like scimitars and whose descriptions of Hell make Dante's *Inferno* sound like Club Med.

WORD STUDY

Air-raid drill: Time for intensive prayer for the souls of the faithful departed, one of whom you may soon become.

Bathroom: A place that you visit twice a day and in which you cannot speak.

Fun: Frivolity; regularly permitted, at least four times a year.

Martyrdom: May be required; to be prepared for.

Nun: Your teacher. *Synonym:* Drill Sergeant.

Playground: The place where you line up to go into school.

Ruler: Teaching aid.

Uniform: What you wear to school no matter how dirty.

37. What are the six parts of a Catholic schoolgirl's uniform?
The six parts of a Catholic schoolgirl's uniform are the shoes, the socks, the jumper, the blouse, the tie and the beanie.

38. What are the three parts of a Catholic schoolboy's uniform?
The three parts of a Catholic schoolboy's uniform are the trousers, the shirt and the tie.

39. Why can't a Catholic schoolchild have his uniform dry-cleaned?
A Catholic schoolchild can't have his uniform dry-cleaned because he must wear it every day.

40. Why do Catholic schoolchildren line up in the playground and march into school in the morning?
Catholic schoolchildren line up and march into school because Sister says to.

41. Why are Catholic schoolrooms crowded?
Catholic schoolrooms are crowded because each child is sharing her desk with her guardian angel.

42. When is a Catholic schoolchild not allowed to talk?

A Catholic schoolchild is almost never allowed to talk. She cannot talk in the halls, in the bathroom, in class, in church, in procession or in an air-raid drill.

43. When can a Catholic schoolchild talk?

A Catholic schoolchild may talk when the class is saying prayers or the Pledge of Allegiance at the beginning of the school day, and may get permission to talk in class by raising his hand to answer a question.

What Is Wrong with This Picture?

1. Chewing bubble gum strictly forbidden, of course. (It was rumored that publics were allowed to.) 2. Solid shirts only, please. 3. Sister rarely smiled, usually only when Monsignor came to visit. 4. Everyone knows filmstrips go "beep." (Note the familiar forbidding image of God the Father.) 5. Development of the embryo?! In a Catholic classroom? 6. Real Catholic classrooms were strictly segregated by sex. 7. Scapulars should be worn inside clothing, not outside. These are signs of devotion and penance, not fashion accents. (Neither are rosaries, which belong in your pocket unless you're a nun.) 8. Children were frequently punished by being sent to stand in the trash can—the Catholic equivalent of a dunce's cap. 9. Erasers were used for more than cleaning blackboards. They also made great "conversation stoppers." 10. Scraps of leftover lunch were put on windowsill for birds and squirrels to eat. It's a sin to waste food.

44. Do Catholic schoolchildren often raise their hands to answer a question?

Catholic schoolchildren rarely raise their hands to answer a question as they are afraid to give the wrong answer.

45. When may a Catholic schoolchild go to the bathroom?

A Catholic schoolchild may go to the bathroom when Sister takes the class to the bathroom, and not until. If an emergency arises, the child can go to the bathroom in his seat.

46. Why do Catholic schoolchildren write neatly and keep clean notebooks?

Catholic schoolchildren write neatly and keep clean notebooks because their belongings are an extension of themselves and they always show respect for their bodies, which are temples of the Holy Ghost.

47. Do Catholic schoolchildren know how to behave toward nuns, priests and in church?

Catholic schoolchildren practice a more elaborate system of behavior than is required of the Chief of Protocol at the Court of St. James.

48. Do Catholic schoolchildren ever get rewarded for being good?

Catholic schoolchildren often get rewarded for being good. Sister gives out prayer books, rosaries, statues, scapulars and other religious articles for good behavior, such as not turning your head during Mass.

49. Do Catholic schoolchildren understand the importance of corporal punishment?

Catholic schoolchildren understand the importance of corporal punishment because they experience it daily.

SOLDIERS OF CHRIST:
THE REQUIRED UNIFORM

hundreds of prayers committed to memory

white tailored blouse, purchased at J.C. Penney; eighth graders will try to get away with pale pink or yellow

green glen plaid jumper with fashionable inverted pleats; handed down from big sister

knee socks that never seem to stay up; rubber bands are used to secure them, cutting off circulation in lower leg

regulation shoes (never black patent leather)

hair getting a little long; should never touch collar or ears

wrinkled white shirt, not striped, checked or colored

Holier Than Thou insignia

offending hand that will soon be rapped; never forget that Sister has eyes in back of her head

khaki trousers (gray and navy blue are also popular), either too long or too short, and baggy enough to accommodate gym shorts for P.E. class

50. Why do Catholic schoolchildren experience corporal punishment?

Catholic schoolchildren experience corporal punishment because they don't always remember things they were assigned to memorize, because they often talk to their neighbors in class and because they sometimes have to go to the bathroom at the wrong time.

51. What do Catholic schoolchildren do for a break from routine?

For a break from routine, Catholic schoolchildren sell Holy Childhood stamps, trade holy cards, sell candy and magazines, buy pagan babies and have air-raid drills.

52. Do Catholic schoolchildren have fun?

Catholic schoolchildren have a lot of fun on St. Blaise Day, in the Christmas pageant and the May Procession and during Lent when they spend Friday afternoons in church saying the Stations of the Cross.

53. Are Catholic schoolchildren prepared for martyrdom?

Catholic schoolchildren are prepared for martyrdom and would be happy to stand up for their faith.

54. Who is likely to ask a Catholic schoolchild to renounce his faith?

The Communists are likely to ask a Catholic schoolchild to renounce his faith because they are committed to defiling the souls of Catholic children.

55. Why do Catholic schoolchildren learn a lot in school?

Catholic schoolchildren learn a lot in school because they are afraid.

NUNS

Tiny First Graders dressed in plaid jumpers or regulation white shirts have little idea of what they are getting into. Known to terrify even the bravest child, from day one nuns are a complete mystery. Some even have men's names. But they are a fact of life for children of the cloth.

Nuns practiced behavior modification ages before it became trendy. Quickly, Sister's students learned to follow her instructions, and thus the path to Heaven, on threats of swats from the ruler for so much as a sideways glance. The good nuns, who jingled their rosary beads to let you know they were coming back into the classroom so they wouldn't catch you misbehaving, were few and far between.

Early in the school year, good girls and boys learn that God or Sister, or both, is always watching, so they do what they're told and nothing else. Shooting spitwads, they quickly learn, is a venial sin, as is drawing a picture of Sister Gabriella with her eyes crossed. Minor infractions such as these can be cleared up with a visit to the confessional, a good Act of Contrition, and buying more pagan babies than anyone else in the class. The prize, a little plastic madonna, is a bonus.

What's in a Name?:
A Nun's Own Story

One day two bright and perky young nuns visited Sister Apollinaria's Seventh Grade class to talk about vocations. As a follow-up the next day, the ancient, somewhat world-weary but kindly Sister Apollinaria decided to hold for her students a question-and-answer session about the religious life. After a predictable series of queries and responses—"Do you miss your family?," "Do you have your own room?," "What's your favorite TV show?"—Sister was clearly tiring and announced that she would take only one more question. One student waved his hand, was recognized and asked, "Are nuns allowed to choose their own names?" Sister sighed, laid her elbows on the desk, slowly leaned forward and said quietly but with feeling, "If nuns were allowed to choose their own names, do you think for *one minute* I would have chosen 'Apollinaria'?"

A NUN'S STORY

eight zillion prayers committed to memory

hair?

rimless glasses

breasts?

prayer book; studied while children are at recess

yardstick kept handy for swatting troublesome children

immaculately clean fingernails

tissue stuffed up sleeve

regulation rosary always ready

sensible black shoes that last for decades

QUESTIONS WE DIDN'T HAVE THE NERVE TO ASK

Do you have hair?

How do you stay cool in the summer?

Do you have breasts?

Could you wear different color shoes if you wanted to?

Are you allowed to drive?

Are you married to a priest?

Do you wear black underwear?

WHAT TO GIVE NUNS FOR CHRISTMAS

Handkerchiefs

Gloves (black only, no beads or feathers)

Hand lotion

Homemade cookies

Mass card you made yourself

Pretty box of stationery (but not *too* pretty)

Scented soap

Box of chocolates

THE MAY PROCESSION

Day hymn, will become trance-like. Sister Mary Homeroom, herself in a state of mystical awe, may well be so preoccupied that the procession, left to its own devices, ends up amid galoshes and raincoats in the cloakroom. A few raps on the knuckles later, the class makes its way to the statue of benevolent Mary. The slightly battered crown is placed reverently upon her head and everyone joins in one last rousing chorus of "O Mary, We Crown Thee with Blossoms Today . . ."

Sometimes a school will go a step further and organize a gala May crowning festival, highlighted by a procession that bears close resemblance to an ancient pilgrimage. Hundreds of chanting, white-robed children parade through the playground, around the school and into the church. As teachers and camera-clutching mothers look on, the Blessed Virgin is crowned. The sweet little girl chosen out of the entire school to do the crowning appears not unlike the winner of a blessed Miss America pageant.

Each May first, parochial schoolchildren line up in their classrooms and "bring flowers of the fairest" to honor Mary, Queen of the May.

One lucky child, often a diminutive blond angel named Mary, leads the procession carrying a tiny woven crown of flowers perched on a small pillow. Up and down the aisles the line snakes. (Yes, line singular. Because of the narrow aisles, boys and girls, just this once, form a co-ed line.)

Often the class, swaying along and chanting the May

FIRST HOLY COMMUNION

Nuns tell you it's the happiest day of your life. Parents beam at you proudly, momentarily forgetting that you broke the lamp playing indoor basketball last week. Greeting cards, often containing money, arrive in the mail for you.

The cause of all the merriment? Your First Holy Communion.

Heart, soul and body have undergone intense preparation for this sacred event. For weeks, catechism class has consisted of pre-Communion drills, to the extent that you can pronounce "transubstantiation" and almost understand what it means. Father has been visiting your First Grade classroom, simulating what will happen on The Big Day. As each name is called, a child walks slowly up to the front of the classroom, hands praying reverently fingertip to fingertip, and head bowed slightly. Then Father places an unconsecrated host on the child's outstretched tongue. After a brief pause and thoughtful Sign of the Cross, the recipient shuffles back to her seat. Some priests are known to practice administering Communion with quarters, reusable host substitutes.

By the day the Day of Days arrives, your class is well rehearsed, yet someone always pees or throws up because of all the excitement. Parents act understandingly, but they're usually annoyed because they've gone to all the trouble of dressing you up. Girls look like little brides of Christ outfitted in pristine dresses and veils, clutching shiny new rosaries, prayer books and pocketbooks. Little boys in white suits seem like nothing less than miniature disco madmen. In the eyes of teachers, parents and relatives, however, on their First Communion Day, all little boys and girls are angels.

DO-IT-YOURSELF PLAY MASS KIT

Catholic children, like any others, need diversions on rainy days. There is no better way to keep youngsters amused, while at the same time instilling traditional Catholic values, than by playing Mass. Parents should not be concerned that Play Mass is sacrilegious. Thousands of priests started out this way.

MATERIALS NEEDED FOR PLAY MASS

Bath towels (Cannon or St. Mary's brands preferred) become colorful priestly vestments. Usually, the eldest male child plays the priest. He wraps a bath towel around his waist and drapes another over his back, securing it in front with a big safety pin. Younger siblings, male or female, attend as altar boys. They may also wear towels, although this is optional.

A *card table* is easily transformed into the altar. Cover with a sheet and decorate with Sick-Call crucifix set, a Bible, and salad-dressing cruets.

A *shoe box* covered with a hand towel makes a fine tabernacle.

A *goblet* filled with grape juice adds a special touch. The children are much too young to drink wine.

Hosts may be created from a number of foods. Remember, since Communion is generally the highlight of Play Mass, it may be administered a dozen or more times during the course of the ceremony. So make the hosts authentic but tasty. Necco Wafers and circles cut out of squashed slices of Wonder bread are suggested.

A *kazoo*, hummed reverently, inspires hearty singing.

A band of kazoos, playing "Holy God We Praise Thy Name" in rounds, makes a rousing Play Mass finale.

An outdoor variation of Play Mass is Play Funeral Mass, which requires deceased birds or insects. The tiny carcasses are wrapped in paper towels, placed in cardboard "caskets" and buried in the backyard. Graves are marked with flowers from Mom's garden and crosses constructed from Popsicle sticks.

SOLDIERS OF CHRIST

Confirmation is almost as big a production as First Holy Communion. Once again, there are special instructions, and recipients may be required to don special clothes: red gowns this time for the boys, perennial white for girls. Once again, youngsters parade down the aisles of the parish church with beaming parents, relatives and friends in attendance. Best of all, the confirmed get the chance to pick yet another Christian name, as compensation for having had no choice at Baptism.

As the name implies, the purpose of Confirmation is to *confirm* Catholics already baptized in their faith. They even repeat the same words that were spoken on their behalf at Baptism by their godparents. "Do you renounce Satan?" "I do renounce him." "And all his works?" "I do renounce them." And so forth, until you lay that devil down.

The Church requires an adult sponsor for each of the newly confirmed, to guide them in the development and practice of their faith. Godparents make the ideal candidates, since their responsibilities will be along the same lines as before. However, any Good Catholic will do.

Confirmation takes place periodically at each parish, depending upon the Bishop's schedule. The candidates are generally youngsters between the ages of eight and fourteen, and converts. A Bishop performs the ceremony because he is considered to be a direct spiritual successor of the Apostles. Like much else in the Catholic Church, Con-

---

If the Name Fits

Confirmation is justifiably the favorite sacrament of many Catholics, entirely because they are allowed to select a new, additional name. If neither your first nor your middle name pleases you, this is your chance to start anew, so don't get bogged down by tradition.

Your Confirmation name must be a saint's name, so pull out *Lives of the Saints* and let your imagination soar! A wisely chosen Confirmation name gives you opportunities galore. Owning four initials can only help you secure invitations to the right dinner parties. In her caviar-and-vodka days, for example, Susan A. Miller takes to signing her name S. Anastasia Miller. With his highbrow Confirmation name, David Thomas Sebastian Rhodes sounds more like a shipping magnate than a just-confirmed paper boy.

A well-meaning adult may encourage you to take the name of your grandfather or favorite nun. DON'T BE TEMPTED! This is your once-in-a-lifetime chance to choose a new name without undergoing complicated legal proceedings, so don't blow it. Grandpa Herman and Sister Mathilda will understand.

Try on names the way you do hats. And, as with hats, try to determine if your Confirmation name will be fashionable, or at least wearable, in twenty years. Personal qualities often point to that perfect Confirmation name. Here are a few character traits and names that suit them:

Flamboyant: *Yves, Veronica, Ingrid, Zita, Bibiana, Salome*
Traditional: *Joseph, Mary, John, Elizabeth*
Brave: *Daniel, Joan*
Whimsical: *Felicity, Elmo, Sylvester, Felix*
Doubtful: *Thomas*
Serious: *Scholastica, Ethelbert, Pythias, Bonaventure*
Cool: *Fabian*

If you have gotten the calling, names like Chastity, Pius, Perpetua and Boniface are fine. Otherwise, make another selection.

firmation is a commemoration of something that once happened to the Apostles.

Shortly after the first Easter Sunday, the Apostles were seated in a locked room when they received a sign that the Holy Ghost was about to descend upon them. Apparently God could not spare a messenger angel that day. Instead, a great wind blew outside, small tongues of fire appeared on the heads of the Apostles and they began to speak in foreign languages. *Now* you know how the Holy Ghost got His name.

Nowadays, the prospective confirmed do not expect the Holy Ghost to appear as tongues of fire above their heads unless they have been doused with Sterno. Nor do they anticipate being able to quote scripture in perfect Swahili. Instead, the Bishop will lay his hand on the head of each person to be confirmed, make the Sign of the Cross on the recipient's forehead with holy oil and give him a slight blow on the cheek.

The confirmed Catholic must be ready at any time to profess his faith, to practice it fearlessly as a soldier of Christ and perhaps (the blow on the cheek) even to die for it. To help the newly confirmed, the Holy Ghost bestows seven gifts upon them: wisdom, understanding, counsel, fortitude, knowledge, piety and fear of the Lord.

Thus, Confirmation helped give Mr. and Mrs. Murray the fortitude to decline smilingly the meat course at the home of their non-Catholic friends the Johnsons one Friday night. Other virtues prevented Mr. Murray from muttering under his breath, "The inconsiderate fools—this is the second Friday this has happened in the past three months!" These virtues are presumably wisdom, counsel and fear of Mrs. Murray.

Is It a Bird?

The Holy Ghost is one third of the Holy Trinity. (The other two thirds are God the Father and God the Son, who is also known as Jesus Christ.) Beyond this, little is known. Is the Holy Ghost a dove, wind or fire? He, She or It? Catholics believe in things they have never seen, felt, or heard, and they believe most deeply in things they have never been able to figure out.

FATHER WHAT-A-WASTE

In every Catholic schoolgirl's life there appears at one time or another a young, handsome stranger. He is friendly, warm, sincere and listens willingly to her problems. He "understands" her as no one ever has. He even plants a little kiss on her cheek when he comes to her family's house while conducting the parish census; it's to die from. But there's only one fly in the holy ointment: he is a priest, and his name is Father What-a-Waste.

Father What-a-Waste comes from Topeka, Kansas, was the captain of the state championship basketball team, never kissed a girl on the first date—or the second, for that matter—and has now, of course, forsworn such pleasures entirely.

He is devoted to his mother; his family thinks he's a saint. Once, when Miller's pond had barely frozen over, Bingo, the What-a-Waste family dog, ventured onto the ice while chasing a rabbit. The paper-thin surface began to give way, and thirteen-year-old Father What-a-Waste plunged into the frigid water to rescue his beloved pet. He offered up to the poor souls in Purgatory the three days he spent in the hospital with hypothermia.

The parishioners fawn over Father What-a-Waste, and the St. Cleo's High School Broncos never had a better coach. In short, everyone loves Father What-a-Waste, but no one more than the girls of Sister Theresa's Eighth Grade class. He strides into the classroom like Robert Redford in a Roman collar. As he looks from one fresh young face to another, hearts melt, and even

Sister smiles beatifically as Father What-a-Waste explains that more dented cans of vegetables than ever are needed for this year's Catholic Relief Services' drive.

The girls normally take little interest in sports. But when Father What-a-Waste shoots baskets with the boys at recess, they show more enthusiasm than the Dallas Cowboy cheerleaders, squealing with glee when he hits twenty-foot jumpers in full cassock. As the bevy flocks to Father What-a-Waste's side, he straightens his collar, checks his reflection in the school window and quickly smooths down his hair. Father What-a-Waste never has any idea of his effect on his spiritual charges—or does he?

VOCATION DAY:
Getting the Calling

Once a year, Catholic children are called upon to consider whether or not they have a vocation. They make posters extolling the religious life, and nuns and priests come in to talk to them about

its glorious rewards. Although everyone happily pays lip service to how wonderful it would be to be chosen by God, in truth, the thought that you could get the calling was horrifying.

Even though at some point in their parochial school career every Catholic boy and girl wanted to be a priest or a nun, it was usually only a passing fancy and a desire to wear nuns' clothes, see the inside of the convent or rectory or peek into the tabernacle. But the calling was the real thing and a serious threat to life as we knew it.

The calling usually came in the form of a tap on the shoulder. If you were called it meant you had an undeniable vocation, and the worst thing about it was that you were supposed to want it. You had to hope for it, pray for it and consider yourself lucky if you got it. So what you did when you thought you heard a voice in the night was to close your eyes and pretend you were sleeping; and if you thought you felt a tap, you looked around and hoped to hell you didn't see Christ or the Blessed Mother or a saint with her heart exposed.

Lucky for most of us, the calling was a mosquito or a brother or sister in the next bed, but if it was ever the real thing, we hoped God wouldn't be mad at us for pretending we didn't notice, and would catch us later if He really meant it.

GOING MY WAY? *A VISIT TO THE SEMINARY*

If you are an Eighth Grade boy and you didn't get the calling on your own, a visit to the seminary is in order.

All the boys are loaded into cars and driven to the nearest seminary, where their priest introduces them to their guide. Why it's Johnny Frankenelli, the best-looking, best basketball player and nicest guy from your older brother's Eighth Grade class, and, boy, does he look happy. He enthusiastically describes the routine at the seminary: the hours of prayer—morning, noon and night; the hours spent studying—morning, noon, and night. He takes great pains to show you the great gym you can use if you can find the time before 4:30 A.M. or after midnight.

Since this excursion is usually an exercise in futility in getting you to want to become a priest, no one feels too bad about the fact that very few boys ever join. After all, if you had the calling, they wouldn't be driving you out for a visit anyway.

CCD VERSUS PAROCHIAL SCHOOL:
Point-Counterpoint

Catholic children who do not attend parochial school are required to take religious instruction on a weekday afternoon or Saturday morning. These classes are known as CCD (Confraternity of Christian Doctrine). The following is the testimony of two Catholic schoolboys, eleven years old, one a CCDer and the other a parochial school student.

POINT

CCDer: I hate to give up Saturday mornings to go to CCD, but I'd rather do that than go to Catholic school—that place is weird!

The desks are old and stupid, the books are old and stupid, everything's old and stupid—the pencils, the blackboards, the whole building! They don't even have any AV equipment! But it's kind of fun going through other people's desks—what else is there to do, anyway, before the stupid teacher gets there?

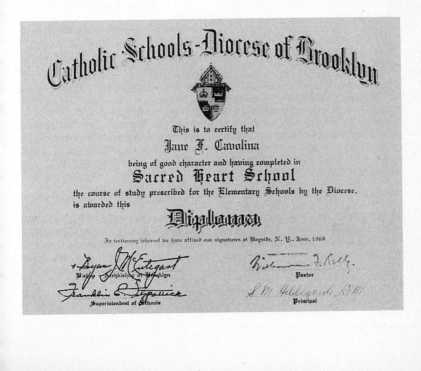

Catholic Schools - Diocese of Brooklyn

This is to certify that
Jane F. Cavolina
being of good character and having completed in
Sacred Heart School
the course of study prescribed for the Elementary Schools by the Diocese, is awarded this
Diploma

In testimony whereof we have affixed our signatures at Bayside, N. Y., June, 1968

Bishop Archbishop of Brooklyn

Superintendent of Schools

Pastor

Principal

COUNTERPOINT

My cousin goes to Catholic school and she knows all the Holy Days of Obligation by heart. Who cares? All I know is that my parents make me go to church on weekdays sometimes. Sundays are bad enough. My cousin says the nuns hit people over the knuckles with rulers if they don't have the right answers. If a teacher ever did that to me at my school, my father would sue. Every once in a while, though, my mother does threaten to send me to Catholic school. My father doesn't like nuns, and he says why should he pay taxes to support the public schools and pay for a Catholic school too?

Just before I made my first Communion, I had to take a whole day off from my school for extra CCD classes. My teacher didn't like it very much and said she was glad we had separation of Church and state in America. But she's prejudiced because she's Protestant. I know because when she says the Our Father in class she says, "For thine is the kingdom and the power and the glory, for ever and ever. Amen," at the end. My mother says not to say that part.

PAROCHIAL SCHOOL STUDENT: I'm sure glad I go to Catholic School, 'cause if I didn't I'd have to go to CCD classes. They actually have to go on Saturday. It's bad enough you gotta go to church on Sunday. Sometimes when we're playing ball in the field behind the school you can see them sitting there at our desks—they look so sad. Sometimes they come to church, too, but I'm not sure they're really Catholic. If they are, how come they don't go to our school?

On Monday when you go to your desk you always find stuff missing or broken or messed up. The erasers that we cleaned on Friday are all full of chalk and the blackboard is all written on. If you break something during the week, though, you can blame it on the CCDers.

My friend Joey goes to public school and has to go to CCD classes, but he's just learning stuff we had way back in First Grade. And he hasn't even made First Communion yet! My mom and dad really want me to go to Catholic school and don't mind paying for it since you get a better education there.

ST. SCHOLASTICA HIGH SCHOOL

St. Scholastica appears no different from any other suburban high school—manicured lawns dotted with an occasional Coke can, well-equipped facilities, a fine gymnasium. But while their public counterparts are saluting the flag, reciting the Pledge of Allegiance and listening to a recitation of the lunch menu on the P.A., St. Scholastica students are still kneeling with heads bowed twenty minutes into their morning geometry class. Evolution is a topic barely breezed through in biology. And there are only two acceptable outfits: an unfashionable plaid skirt and white blouse for girls and a pale-blue shirt, black tie and crisp navy blue pants for boys. St. Scholastica students wear uniforms for the same reason the Rockettes do—so that everyone looks equal, though in this case equally bad.

Religion classes are required every semester and pupils are allowed to select from a variety of traditional offerings—Old Testament, New Testament, Scripture—as well as several "relevant" courses designed and titled to appeal to a teen's modern lifestyle: "Search for Self," "Today's Catholic, Rights and Responsibilities," and "Jesus Is in You and Me." The relevance of these new-fangled courses escapes the students, who sit listlessly through them with the same ennui as others do their class in New Testament. There is one notable exception. Everyone at St. Scholastica will at one time or another enroll in Sister Sarah's "Bible as Literature" course. Its popularity and notoriety can be attributed to the fact that Sister Sarah finds it appropriate a couple of times a year to interject her lectures with random bits of sex education. No one ever misses a class, hoping that today is the day the seniors have been telling them about all year long when Sister Sarah will take out specially colored chalk and draw the male and female reproductive organs on the blackboard.

St. Scholastica's students anticipate the school-sponsored dances with relish, and no time more than after the St. Scholastica Scholars have scored the winning touchdown in the last seconds of the game against their arch rivals, the St. Sebastian Arrows, and the postgame victory dance becomes a frenzy of celebration. Mingling affably through the throngs of gyrating teenage bodies are the chaperones, Father Vince and Sister Mary Anne. Their presence is hardly noticed until, during a rare slow dance, Father Vince taps the wide-receiver-turned-dancer on the shoulder and reminds him to leave room for the Holy Ghost between him and his cheerleader girlfriend. Sister Mary Anne stands by the punch bowl and blinks rapidly during the slow numbers. Only those students who are running for student council or who plan to ask Sister Mary

Anne for a recommendation for college applications will stop to chat. The subjects of conversation will consist of highlights of the football game and the new chipped-beef dish the cafeteria ladies concocted last week.

A UNIFORMED GIRL'S GUIDE TO FASHION

As a parochial school girl, you must take care in selecting a school whose uniform is consistent with your own fashion statement. Once enrolled, your freedom is limited to changing the color of your socks, and this only in the more liberal parochial schools.

By the time you're off to high school and your friends are poring over fall fashion magazines, you want more

THE GIRLS OF ST. SCHOLASTICA

1.

2.

3.

4.

5.

1. Floozie: Will probably be expelled when Father next visits class.

2. Nuns raise their eyebrows at her. Popular with cool boys.

3. If Sister catches her Scotch-taping up her hem, she will be doomed to spending rest of year in knee-length skirt.

4. Friends suspect she has the calling.

5. Practically a nun.

than offbeat argyles to enhance your uniform. Yes, it's a challenge. Yet despite parochial restraints, it is entirely possible for you plaid-clad schoolgirls to evolve into the sort of bon ton sophisticates you dream of becoming. Lucky you if your school's dress regulations are few. Otherwise, not to worry. You will most likely have to accrue several stylistic misjudgments before you are expelled. The idea is to appear outrageous enough to raise eyebrows, but not so outrageous as to be sent to the principal's office. So be reckless. Be daring. Here is what you must do:

1. If a girl had to stake her fashion savior-faire on just one item it would be leggings. Don't be shy about indulging in snazzy black fishnets and green glitter knee socks. Remember, those lackluster frocks have stifled your savvy, so feel free to think of whimsical leg gear as a way of evening out the score.

2. Ditto footwear. Step out in red shoes whenever possible. Anything with a pointy toe and high heel is nice too. For gym class, plain black tennis shoes suggest an air of mystery. Novelty shoelaces are not haute.

3. The application of make-up is one instance that belies the old proverb "more is more." It's hard to get away with much embellishment, as nuns tend to take one look and send you off to the bathroom to scrub your face. By keeping your arms folded, however, you can often offset scrutiny for several days while wearing strangely colored fingernail polish.

4. Forget thin gold chains and sweet pearl earrings, and throw away that charm bracelet you received for your sixteenth birthday. No one forgets the girl who strides boldly into ancient history class sporting slave bracelets, armlets and wrist cuffs. For a *cause célèbre* in the cafeteria, drape thick metal chains around your upper torso. Your local hardware store stocks them in a variety of styles and weights and, best of all, they're reasonably priced.

5. Invent a hairdo that announces *your* fashion statement. Ask your best friend's older sister to show you how to tease your hair. Then use hairspray. Lots. Or clip little velvet bows on your head the way Sally

Rogers did on *The Dick Van Dyke Show*. And don't forget, inexpensive wigs can be stunning.

6. You've reached a plateau in panache. The next step is to see how far your school's dress-code regulations will stretch. On a day you're feeling a tiny bit blue, don a pale pink blouse in lieu of regulation whites and hum the folk Mass version of "Allelieu" all day. If your uniform is a jumper, snip off the bodice and presto— a smart skirt. Roll up the waistband to micro-mini level, or bring a roll of Scotch tape and a friend into the bathroom and create the same effect. At this level, fashion is irrelevant. It's style we're after.

SEX EDUCATION

By high school, the nuns were teaching the girls sex education; that is, that their bodies were temples of the Holy Ghost. Period. The wall between the boys' school and the girls' school kept them from further revelation.

To offset the obvious shortcomings in their knowledge on this point and to ensure that they would behave like good Catholic women when they discovered the hidden truth on their own, Father would visit from time to time to have a real heart-to-heart. (The boys were left to fend for themselves; besides, it was up to the girls to say when too much was enough.)

Father usually addressed the assembly—a few hundred blossoming young girls crowded into the school auditorium. They were then told *exactly* what they could do without committing a grievous sin, and, mostly,

exactly what they couldn't do. As a result, they learned about an awful lot of things they hadn't yet thought of and blushed enough to make the room look like the Red Sea.

If conscience wasn't enough of a guide while out on a date, there was a host of celestial guardians on hand.

THE RETREAT

There are two basic kinds of retreats, the old-style contemplative retreat and the modern interpersonal retreat. The old-style retreat, which is favored by most of the religious and the exceptionally devout, usually lasts anywhere from a weekend to a week. Any longer than that and the retreat is no longer a retreat. You have become a hermit.

The old-style retreat takes place at a wooded, secluded abbey or convent and the days are spent walking in natural beauty while busily fingering a rosary. It is better not to speak to anyone, with the exception of small animals one meets in the woods, in order to maintain a reflective state of mind. Meals are taken

in spartan surroundings. They are bland and not particularly filling, but this isn't The Four Seasons. It is a place where you can think about what a terrible person you are and, one hopes, get your act together enough to be a better person when you leave. While on the old-style retreat you will see some terribly religious people wandering aimlessly (sometimes into trees or small streams) with a look of perfect contentment on their faces. Try to be like them.

The modern retreat is for the more worldly, yet involved, religious and for high school students who cannot be quiet for ten minutes, much less a weekend. These retreats take place at a wooded, secluded brother house, tucked far enough away in the hills or wheat fields that there is no easy access to a liquor depot where a six pack (or worse) could be purchased. The purpose of the retreat for high school students is to try one more time—and in their own language—to get them to think about their role as Catholics in the modern world.

As soon as they arrive at the brother house, which is a large wooden building not unlike a ski lodge, even if it's in the middle of Iowa, the seniors begin plotting how they will get out that night without getting caught. They are unsure how much punishment they may receive if caught, but this makes it all the more exciting. They are then divided into two groups, boys and girls, and shown to their monk-like cells. They find it strange that they should be sequestered in these bare dorms since the rest of the house, with roaring fireplaces and redwood beams, looks like Jerry Ford's condo in Vail.

After orientation, everyone gets together to listen to "Bridge Over Troubled Water." Certain interpersonal games are then played. In one game everyone sits in a big room with a chair in the middle. Each person must take a turn sitting in the chair and anyone can say anything they want to the person in the chair. Usually it is pretty tame stuff; however, every once in a while someone lets loose with, "You know, you seem so stuck up, you don't let anyone get to know you." Whereupon the person in the chair is reduced to tears. Another game involves being forced to select the person in the class you like least and going into the woods or fields with her for an hour without speaking. This exercise is designed to encourage strong friendships.

After three days of mind-boggling and heart-wrenching, everyone gets together and listens to "Bridge over Troubled Water" again, then gets on the bus and sits with the same friends they sat with on the way in, better for the entire experience.

After a modern retreat of this nature one boy will decide to become a priest or brother, two girls who were going to become Sisters decide not to, one boy has a nervous breakdown and three get suspended for drinking beer.

FOUR MORE YEARS

If you do decide to go to college, you will certainly want to make it a Catholic one. Why? The value. *Value in education.* Since the traditions of the teaching orders are deeply rooted in educating themselves to educate you, instead of making money or raising families or having sex, the education you get will be of superior quality. *Value in values.* Catholic colleges are intent upon making sure that the Catholic values you learned as a child are reinforced in the context of the modern-day world—in a word, relevant. *Value in tuition.* Catholic universities are private so they cost more than state-supported schools; in fact, sometimes the equivalent of an Ivy League school—but then, you're getting so much *more.*

A Catholic college is the right choice if you: a) are wild about football and are accepted at Notre Dame; b) are anxiously looking around for that "right" (read *Catholic*) mate; or c) think you might have the calling but are not quite ready to test the holy waters.

MEETING YOUR MATE
Catholic Style

Since you've been raised in the Catholic tradition, when the time comes to select a husband or wife, the Church hopes you will opt for a partner of the same persuasion. If you feel you must comply, there are a host of methods for finding that special Catholic someone.

A few suggestions: when riding the bus to work, strike up a conversation with the sweet-looking girl you see every day—the one who occasionally tucks a holy card inside the historical romance she's reading, sighs, and gazes out the window. If a wild sort of boy appeals to you, hang out in Irish pubs on St. Patrick's Day, paying special attention to the cute lad dancing a jig on the bar. You may meet the soulmate of your dreams on your vacation to Italy by spending several whole days "browsing" through the Vatican City gift shop. When you're home for the holidays, linger in the vestibule after Mass and hope you run into that smart, funny girl who helped you pass social studies in Seventh Grade. If you find out the new, good-looking accountant in the office is named Mickey Ryan, it's worth sitting next to him at the next sales conference.

One of the best ways to unearth a prospective Catholic spouse, however, is to attend a Catholic (and preferably co-ed) college. Half the battle is won the first day when you realize that it's true—just about everyone there really is Catholic. All you have to do is join the activities and sign up for the classes you think your soon-to-be-beloved might take part in. Even if you freeze when you have to speak up in class, look into the debate club, where the orator of your dreams might be locked away. Go on blind dates whenever you're asked. Smile a lot. Sometimes the strategies work,

sometimes they don't, and sometimes you don't need them. The following is a true

Some Things to Look for When Selecting a Catholic College

1. **Good basketball team.** It is not worth attending Catholic college unless the school's b-ball is nationally ranked.
2. **Male to female ratio.** *For women:* select a college in the big city. Lots of dates, yet your college can remain a refuge against the wicked excesses. *For men:* select a college that has a sister school. Something happens to Catholic girls when they get away from home for the first time.
3. **Availability of bars.** When visiting the campus, check to make sure there is an active bar scene. In rural areas bars should be spaced no more than two hundred feet apart along the college strip. Not a problem in the city.
4. **Dress code.** If you really feel you must; but remember, it's going to be a lot like high school. Maybe that's why you're going to Catholic college anyway.
5. **Athletic facilities.** Most Catholic colleges rival the Dallas Cowboys when it comes to stadia and equipment, but worth checking out just in case.

BEST CATHOLIC COLLEGES FOR SPORTS

1. Notre Dame
2. De Paul
3. Boston College
4. Georgetown
5. St. John's (New York)
6. Gonzaga
7. Siena
8. Villanova
9. Holy Cross
10. Marquette

11. Xavier
12. St. Bonaventure
13. Loyola Chicago
14. Loyola Marymount
15. La Salle
16. Providence
17. Catholic U.
18. Niagara
19. Fairfield
20. Slippery Rock*

*Note. Slippery Rock is *not* a Catholic college, but most Catholic sports fans would like it to be.

story of a typical Catholic couple's meeting.

John and Mary first noticed each other at the kick-off mixer in September. She admired the effortless way he joked around with the priests. He liked her ready smile. At the punch bowl, they introduced themselves and chatted about where they were from and what their majors were. John asked Mary if she would like to go out for a pizza sometime and she said sure. Soon they were studying together and sitting next to each other at football games. They even worked to-

gether on the folk Mass decoration committee, designing imaginative felt banners to be hung behind the altar. By the end of the school year they were inseparable and in love. Their friends knew it was only a matter of time before they became engaged. Sure enough, on graduation day, they announced their intentions to an assemblage of pleased family and friends. Mary's mother was especially delighted; after all, wasn't this the moment she had been ardently awaiting since she packed her daughter off to Notre Dame four years ago?

CATHOLIC COLLEGES THAT DON'T SOUND CATHOLIC

University of Scranton, Scranton, Pennsylvania

New York Literary Institute, New York, New York

Fordham University, New York, New York

St. Louis University, St. Louis, Missouri

Gonzaga University, Spokane, Washington

Spring Hill College, Mobile, Alabama

Loras College, Dubuque, Iowa

Villanova University, Villanova, Pennsylvania

Calvert College, New Windsor, Maryland

University of Dayton, Dayton, Ohio

University of Santa Clara, Santa Clara, California

Manhattan College, New York, New York

Poydras College, Pointe Coupee, Louisiana

University of San Francisco, San Francisco, California

Niagara University, Niagara Falls, New York

Creighton University, Omaha, Nebraska

University of Portland, Portland, Oregon

Iona College, New Rochelle, New York

University of Dallas, Dallas, Texas

Manhattanville College, Purchase, New York

Boston College, Chestnut Hill, Massachusetts

HOLY ROLLO UNIVERSITY
RURAL ROUTE 3
CUSTER, PENNSYLVANIA 22618

Sister Jean Inconsolata Jones, President

Education with a Catholic flair, a career with a tradition—that's Holy Rollo, set in a valley in a small burg in the picturesque rolling hills of western Pennsylvania. The campus consists of three attractive Georgian-style buildings, including a Quonset hut dormitory attractively muraled with scenes from the passion of Our Lord. The campus also features an elegantly gardened quad of natural vegetation. The emphasis is on involvement. The school boasts a newspaper (*Rollo the Presses*) and many extracurricular organizations including the Little Sisters of Rollo, a community service group that helps those in the poor mining town of Shale, forty-five minutes from campus.

The Student Body

Enrollment	301	Age Breakdown:	44.9% under 25
Men:	12		55.1% over 25
Women:	289		
Full-time:	55	Ethnic Breakdown:	
Part-time:	246	White:	300
Graduate:	6	Mission-supported student	
Undergraduate:	295	from Zambia	1

Campus Attractions

- Full service vending-machine dining hall
- The Red Demon Rollers, statewide Division 9 Basketball Champions
- Access to Shale town library
- Literary magazine: *Thoughts, Reflections and Good Feelings*
- Senior Yearbook: *Roll On*

What Will It Cost?

Tuition and Fees: Tuition $23,461.63
                        Room and Board . . . . . . 6,888.30 (Quonset hut)
                                            292.99 (Campsite)

How Can You Pay?

Approximately 99.7% of the students recieve some type of financial aid.

Interested?

A nonrefundable application fee of $375.00 is needed to process your application. Your application must be submitted no later than the first day of the semester the student wishes to attend. May be made verbally or in writing.

Average test scores: Men . . . . SAT combined: 900
                        Women . . . . SAT combined: 1250

A TOEFL score of 200 is needed for students whose native language is
    not English.
A TOEFL score is not required of students who speak in tongues.

Programs

Degrees offered:

B.A.	*Brother of the Arts*
M.B.A.	*Master of Beatification Administration*
B.S.	*Brother of Sciences*
D.H.D.	*Doctor of Honor and Devotions*
M.F.A.	*Master of Fatima Adoration*
J.D.	*Doctor of Jesusology*

III

Our
Parochial
Lives

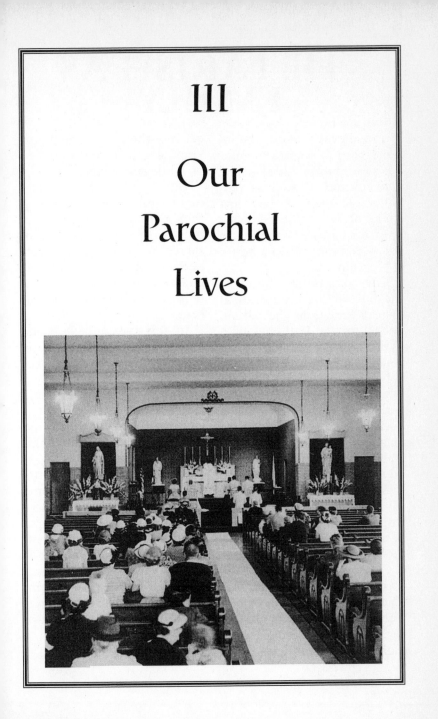

THE PARISH AS FAMILY

In medieval Europe, the local church was the center of community life—social and cultural as well as religious. Though it has lost some of its influence since then, for many a Catholic it is still much more than a house of worship.

The community church is the hub of the ecclesiastical district known as the parish, and all of the Catholics who live within its boundaries are considered to belong to it. Tell a true-blue Catholic what city you live in or come from, and he will ask, "What parish?" The answer is as indicative of socioeconomic status as a Manhattan street address and confers a distinctive identity. "Saint Dom's? My brother married a girl from Saint Dom's." "Holy Family? We used to massacre them in football."

First and foremost, of course, the church is the place where Catholics honor God at Mass. Because Mass is such a rich experience—spiritually, aesthetically and otherwise—there is much to know about it, and much to do while attending.

But it's not only Saturday night and Sunday morning that Catholics frequent the holy precincts. The parish serves a social and recreational function, too, and offers everyone a variety of activities and opportunities to help out.

In this day and age, one might ask, Why must the Church provide these kinds of activities when they are so widely available elsewhere? Because they help create camaraderie and loyalty to the institution, that's why. And because they can be conducted according to the Church's own wholesome standards—not those of a secular world that often seems to be going to Hell in an amoral hand basket.

Remember, "catholic" is a word as well as a religion. The word means all-inclusive, and that means every area of life.

WE GATHER IN HIS NAME

Mass, or more properly the celebration of Mass, is the central ritual in a Catholic's life. Like a good Off-Broadway production, it has a beginning, a middle and, thank goodness, an end. Unlike Off-Broadway, attendance is mandatory, and failure to show up on Sunday or on a Holy Day of Obligation can result in a dreaded mortal sin.

Mass is an opportunity for the priest to lecture the faithful, for the church to collect money for the "new" church that is always in the process of being built and a chance for the latest in fashion to be displayed.

The priest always plays the lead in this production. The choir sings the lyrics, altar boys play the bit parts and the faithful are the audience. As in more avant-garde plays, the audience is encouraged to participate.

The mean-spirited among them wonder what's the earliest you can leave and still fulfill the obligation, but this production has been running for nearly two thousand years.

WHAT'S IN A NAME?
The Most Popular Parish Names

Sacred Heart	Holy Family
St. Mary's	Holy Cross
St. Patrick's	Holy Martyrs
Immaculate Conception	St. Luke's
St. Joseph's	Our Lady of Mount Carmel
St. Anne's	St. Francis of Assisi
Our Lady of the Blessed Sacrament	Annunciation
St. Francis Xavier	Assumption
St. John's	St. Teresa's
Our Lady of Fatima	St. Michael's
St. Peter's	St. Pius X
St. Paul's	St. Mark's
Holy Name	Christ the King

AN ANNOTATED SCHEDULE OF MASSES

The attitude of many young Catholics toward going to Mass parallels their feeling about loss of virginity: might as well get it over with. Admittedly, one discovers later in life that some things *do* bear repeating. Mandatory weekly devotion may simply not be one of them.

Nevertheless, attendance at Mass (and all Holy Days of Obligation) is required behavior. Many of the younger Catholic set think of it as, well, honoring thy father and thy mother.

At least, like an ecclesiastical Baskin-Robbins, the Catholic Church does try to "flavor" one's weekly obligation by offering variety. For instance, at Holier Than Thou parish, one has the option of attending any of the following:

Saturday Afternoon Mass: This "counts" as Sunday; often put into the most straightforward of the "getting it over with" categories. *Pros:* Sleep late on Sunday like the Protestants. *Cons:* Beans and hot dogs must be covered over till after 6:00 P.M. Franks tend to dry out.

Early Morning Mass (7:30 A.M.): For the truly devout. The elderly will be there in quantity; back-row pews chock-a-block full; deep genuflections, two knees. *Pros:* Again, one "gets it over with" early in day; in summer, still time to get to the beach early. Also, one's feelings of piety are strongly enhanced by walking to church in dawn's gray light. Everything will seem slightly mystical. God may "speak" to you in the sunrise. *Cons:* No good for stay-a-beds; also, fashions of elderly communicants can be dreary.

9:00 A.M. Mass (Parochial School Mass): Youngsters are sent to sit with their classes. May not be attended in comfort by anyone over the age of twelve. *Pros:* Parents are free to sleep late and attend later Mass. *Cons:* Parents must have breakfast ready upon the return of ravenous, post-fast youngsters, then worry about what the kids are up to while parents themselves attend Mass.

10:30 A.M. Mass (a.k.a. Family Mass): This is the real round-up service; like Restoration theater, the one where people go to see and be seen. This

Mass features high fashion and high drama: children and babies will act up, causing the occasional smothered chuckle from the congregation. It's a good opportunity to check out how rapidly families are growing. Local politicians will always attend this Mass, arriving slightly tardy and parading their entire well-scrubbed family to the front pew. *Pros:* Dramatic; best "all-around" Mass; choir and all accoutrements. *Cons:* Sort of wrecks schedule for the rest of the day. Lasts longer than all other Masses; may have to shake hands or otherwise greet priest afterward. Especially difficult the same week of a particularly grueling session in the confessional. One would never suspect Father of violating his pledge of secrecy, but that doesn't make looking him in the eye any easier.

5:00 P.M. Mass (Sunday): What can we say? You've wrecked your whole day. You can't make up your mind whether to go or not to go; it doesn't sit right after a day of fun and frolic, but you have no plans for the evening. Always sparsely attended. Others have elected to forgo Sun-

day Mass, choosing a state of mortal sin over this dreary exercise. For losers only. *Pros:* If you do drag yourself in, you avoid a state of mortal sin. Also, you are entitled to feel righteous. You went. *Cons:* Narcolepsy, ennui. This is always a no-frills Mass—no organ, no choir, sometimes no altar boys! The priest has already delivered his best sermon of the day and knows you are in no mood to hear it anyway.

FAVORITE EXCUSES FOR NOT GOING TO MASS

Mass may be the Church's central mystery and all that, and so important that failure to attend can bring on the dark blight of mortal sin to putrefy one's soul. At times, it even produced a sense of moral superiority: if other peoples' religions were as high up the celestial ladder as ours, why didn't they have to go to services every week too?

Nevertheless, the Sunday obligation more often engenders feelings of envy and deprivation than smug complacency. On a beautiful Sunday morning, why is everyone else free to head off to the beach, the playground, the ski slopes, or the ball park while Catholics have to go to church? At times, this wondering feeling becomes overpowering for all but the most devout Catholics and necessitates the making up of excuses for not attending Mass.

Call them reasons, call them justifications, call them explanations, call them what you will. They are mostly lies, damned lies, and everyone knows this. In the interest of gentility, however, and in the Christian spirit of giving the sinner the benefit of the doubt, they shall here be called excuses.

1. *Traveling.* Across the ocean, across the state, across town.
2. *Under the weather; not feeling quite up to it.* Plain and simple. Not to be confused with "inclement weather." (See below.)
3. *Too much weekend.* Watched televised *Mass for Shut-Ins* late Sunday morning in pj's. Could not get out of bed.
4. *Attended nuptial Mass on Saturday.* By rights, this should count for Sunday.
5. *Rebellion.* You turn 18 and declare you are old enough to make your own decisions.
6. *Inclement weather.* Varies as to region and season. Snowstorms; bridge out in flood; icy roads; tidal wave; hurricane; earthquake; severe hail. At least you've experienced one "act of God."
7. *For children only.* "Our parents got drunk at a party last night and didn't get up in time to take us to Mass."

THE ASSEMBLED MULTITUDE
Where to Sit in Church

From the point of view of the Roman Catholic Church, the most important decision any Catholic can make on Sunday is the decision to go to Mass. From the point of view of Your Church, however—your family, friends, neighbors, the vestryman—it is perhaps where you decide to sit once you get there. (A notable exception—for the pastor and the members of the parish council, it is how much money you give.)

The range of possibility is extensive and surprisingly subtle. After you've entered the church, dipped the fingers of your right hand into the holy water font and blessed yourself, glance toward the front of the church. The first few pews are not so much the province of the catatonically devout as one might expect, though entranced communicants may certainly be found there. Rather, they are the preserve of the establishment, the upper crust, the pillars of the community, the arrivés and the arrivistes. Here are the doctor, the dentist, the town councilman, the vice-president for marketing, the bank manager, the undertaker, the priest's visiting parents, the organist's husband. For most of the faithful, then, an unacceptable choice—even reasonably devout Catholics will blanch at the notion of religious sacrifice of this magnitude—except in a pinch.

Now turn your attention toward the back of the church, the last pews. These form the humble refuge of the young mothers vainly trying to quiet mewling babes in arms; of those who arrive late and leave early; of the generally marginal Catholics.

For young parents, the soundproof "baby room" at the back of the church is an appealing alternative, equally attractive to those members of the congregation who do not make active use of it. The baby room, generally constructed during the baby boom, is usually found in suburban churches. Thanks to its thick plate glass window and tinny-sounding speaker, children may pretend that the priest is on television. Clearly, the baby room is a situational choice, dictated by temporary circumstances—though for many Catholic mothers "temporary" may begin to feel "endless." Again, unsuitable for most members of the flock.

No, for the normal Mass-goer, the choice is almost always a middle pew in the middle section—a position neither boasting nor slighting of one's devotion and social standing.

Mildly delinquent teenagers have the option of remaining in the vestibule until they leave early, along with the rest of the cool standees—the smokers, the hoods, the greasers. Or they may simply line up leaning against the back wall, hands behind them. In either location, they must not betray, by word or by look, any level of involvement with what is going on around them.

Once a year, even the CYO president is required to observe Mass from the vestibule to prove that he is just one of the guys and not overly sissified by his participation in a church organization. The coolest teenagers of all will steadfastly refuse to enter the church proper even when the priest, who was formerly a chaplain in the marines, booms out for all to hear, "There are plenty of seats right down front, boys." An uneasy silence not normally part of the liturgy will follow.

One can speculate on where these young people will be sit-

How to Use Holy Water

Upon entering the church, you can usually locate a holy water font, inside of which may or may not repose a reddish sponge.

Touch your fingers to the surface of the water, or press your fingertips lightly into the sponge (with your right hand) and make the Sign of the Cross (forehead, sternum, left shoulder, right shoulder). Obviously, you are not looking for quantity here; rather, one should approach the holy water font with all the delicacy and manner one might use with finger bowls. It's the same principle, really.

If you notice that the sponges in your church's fonts are really dried out, it's a thoughtful gesture to let your priest or vestryman know.

Drinking holy water is frowned upon, as is the excessive "user"—the person who walks into church with holy water running in small rivulets down his forehead. This is the same person who will gulp down a more than adequate sip of consecrated wine at Communion.

Many churches have bottled holy water available for the parishioners to purchase—though sometimes it can be had for free, and sometimes for a small contribution. You can, if you like, install holy water fonts in your own home. It's a nice touch and does cut down on sticky fingerprints on the woodwork. Insist that all small children bless themselves upon entering your home.

ting in years hence, in a way that they, too young to be aware of the great circular pattern that is life, would scoff at. Ten years after his vestibule days, the CYO president will be a successful salesman with a pretty wife and two attractive children, all firmly ensconced in the middle pews, next to the former smokers, hoods and greasers and their children. Twenty years later, the CYO president will have made vice-president of his company and will occupy the second-to-front pew with his wife. His younger son—the one who still comes to church—will be standing in the vestibule.

Once you've made the decision to attend Mass, braved the elements to get to the church, chosen the seat suitable to your mood and station in life, executed a proper Sign of the Cross, genuflected respectfully but without attracting undue attention to yourself, knelt and sent a brief, sincere prayer of greeting wafting heavenward, it's time to relax a bit before the show begins.

Survey the fashion parade and confirm that from the pillbox popularized by Jackie Kennedy through a wide assortment of Easter bonnets (if 'tis the season), to sporty white chapel caps, the seductive black-lace mantilla, and even—in a pinch—Kleenex, the Catholic laywoman's hat is her main fashion accent.

Determine which families have new babies and which teenage children have stopped accompanying their parents to Mass. Study the cover of the new missalette and decide whether you think it is more or less attractive than last month's. Try to remember how long that handsome young couple have been coming to church together now. Take a stab at whether the strangers in the pew in front of you are out-of-towners or new parishioners. But first, last, and whenever other amusements pall, read the bulletin. It will give you the official word on what's happening, as well as the vital statistics of the parish.

Keep it handy throughout Mass. It may prove invaluable during an interminable sermon, or when your store of devotion runs out early during the contemplative silence following Communion.

Genuflecting

Genuflecting may be thought of as a courtesy gesture, a way of saying hi to God. "I'm here, and I'm glad to be in Your house."

Within the rather simple constructs of this gesture, Catholics have developed a whole range of mannerisms. The genuflector can exhibit an entire array of attitudes, from arrogant/casual to downright servile.

Having chosen the pew in which she wishes to sit, the proper genuflector goes down on one knee only (the right, of course!) for a duration of *no longer than thirty seconds.* She makes the Sign of the Cross properly (hitting all the designated spots) and gazes straight ahead at the tabernacle—sincerely, but *not* fixedly or obsessively. She returns to a proper posture, enters the pew and kneels for a few moments of silent prayer. Again, this is not to be overdone.

As we've pointed out, genuflectors run the gamut. Let's talk about just two ends of the spectrum, each equally irritating to the Normal Mass-goer.

1. *Mr. or Ms. Sloppy:* Usually makes a hurried entrance to the church—late. Bobs knee down halfway to floor and makes a breezy Sign of the Cross, as if brushing flies away. Tumbles headlong into pew, and usually omits short prayer of greeting once seated. Overall, this nonchalant attitude does not sit well with God.

2. *Mr. or Ms. Ultra-Pious:* We all know the type. Sometimes they fold down into a full-kneel position, both knees on the floor. They bless themselves repeatedly, beat their breasts and stare pensively at the altar. Everything is a Big Deal. They remain in this fixed position seemingly forever. Then, they rise oh-so-slowly, and slide (still staring ahead) into the pew, thence to fall down on the kneelers to enter another trance. Many of the elderly fall into this category. It's depressing and obsequious. In any case, God is *not* impressed by all this bowing and scraping. (And you look more like a Muslim than a Catholic!)

It is simple and easy to master the mechanics of proper genuflection. While this greeting, like a handshake, will tell God a lot about what kind of person you really are, it is nothing to overdo. Daily practice at an exercise barre, proper posture, and (most important) the right attitude are the most essential elements of learning to genuflect. Practice will make perfect!

N.B.: Catholics are required to genuflect whenever passing the tabernacle, whether they are inside or outside a church. Because of the awkwardness of so doing when riding past a church in a bus or a car, or when walking down the street, the short form of genuflection—the simple Sign of the Cross—is totally acceptable in those cases.

Holier Than Thou Parish

Milwaukee, Wisconsin

Rev. Msgr. Patrick McGillicuddy, Pastor
Rev. John Kovalski, Associate Pastor
Rev. Fred Anciento, In Residence

Sr. Robert Ann Reprimando, R.S.M., School Principal
Sr. Sacred Heart of Jesus Farinet
Sr. Mary Magdalene Ruley
Sr. Teresa Furgeson

Mrs. Annabelle Flanagan, Recotry Housekeeper
Mrs. Louise Pulmonaski, Organist and Choir Director

Mass Schedule

Saturday Evenings: 6:00 p.m.
Sundays: 7:30, 9:00, 10:30 a.m., 5:00 p.m.
Holy Days of Obligation: 6:45, 8:00, 10:00 am, 12:00 noon,
                          5:30, 8:00 p.m.
Mass in Polish: Third Wednesday of each month at 7:00 p.m.

Baptisms

Baptisms take place at the Baptismal Font in the back of the
church the second Sunday of the month. Arrangements should
be made at the Rectory nine months in advance. Godparents
must be practicing Catholics. Both parents and Godparents
are required to meet with the priest for a "Jordan Conference"
in advance of the Baptism.

Marriages

Arrangements for marriage ceremonies must be made at the
Rectory at least six months in advance, in order to guarantee
the date and time desired. The nuptial Mass is the highly
recommended form of celebrating Christian marriage and should
be strongly considered when planning the wedding. Attendance
at pre-Cana conferences is required.

Devotions

Miraculous Medal Devotion, Nocturnal Adoration, Our Mother of
Perpetual Help Devotion, Fatima Devotion, First Fridays,
Novenas. Check with Father Fred for details of these devo-
tions, which are open to all members of our parish family.

NOTICE THE DIFFERENCE?

Thanks go to Sister Mary Magdalene's Sixth grade class, who devoted one lunch hour per week in parish upkeep this past month. The shiny pews, well-dusted statues, and smudge-free windows have never looked better. Now that the children appreciate how much work goes into keeping our church looking its best, perhaps such cleanups will be necessary less frequently.

SPORTS NEWS FROM THE ALL-CATHOLIC BASKETBALL LEAGUE

All Saints Massacres St. John the Baptist, 84 - 55

Holy Family Mauls St. Perpetua, 75 - 43

St. Scholastica Whips St. Regina, 94 - 82

Holy Ghost Crucifies Christ the King, 102 - 27

MOTHER'S CLUB DOINGS

An Easter Bake Sale will be held next Saturday in the school cafeteria from 10:00 a.m. to 5:00 p.m. The proceeds will enable the Mother's Club to purchase a much-needed photocopier for the school. Sister Teresa, though cheerfully enduring the vagaries of our old mimeograph machine, is getting a little tired of being asked about her blue thumb! So please come and treat your family to some delectable Easter goodies -- well deserved after Lenten restraint.

WELCOME NEW PARISHIONERS!

After several months of "friendly deliberations" between Holier Than Thou, St. Agatha's, and the Bishop's personal mediator in charge of parish boundary questions, it has been decided that Catholic residents of the new Lazy Days sub-division (and we hear there are many!) will be able to register at either parish. It seems that even though Lazy Days is closer to Holier Than Thou, there has been a cost overrun in the construction of St. Agatha's new parish center, and more parishioners are needed to "shoulder the burden."

We would like to invite all prospective parishioners of Holier Than Thou to attend our special coffee hour after next Sunday's 10:30 a.m. Mass to tour our fine church and school facilities. Father McGillicuddy will talk about plans for our wholly pre-financed parish center (ground-breaking ceremonies next spring!), which will relieve the slight overcrowding we have recently been experiencing.

PARISH COLLECTION RESULTS

Last week's regular collection: $2,359.27

Last week's special collection for the missions of Upper Volta: $5,398.91
(An all-time missionary collection high!)

We are pleased that Father Swamambi's moving appeal inspired you to give so generously to Upper Volta's needy missions. Such generosity to unfortunate people in faraway lands can only motivate us to recognize our obligations to our own parish family.

ST SCHOLASTICA HIGH NEWS

Members of St. Scholastica High School's Girls Wrestling Team will sponsor a car wash and tire rotation service in the church parking lot today after all Masses. Requested donation is $5.00 and the proceeds will go towards new knee-pads and travel expenses for the statewide Catholic tourney. A dashboard statuette of St. Perpetua (the team's patron saint) will be provided free to each customer. Bring your car by and help the girls bring home another trophy.

MARK YOUR CALENDAR

Preparations are underway for the Polish-American Heritage Association's annual "Spring Fling," to be held on May 19 from 8:00 p.m. to midnight at the K of C hall. Donations are $10.00 per couple and reservations can be made by calling Betty Csarcyks at 665-5414. The theme this year will be "Happiness Is . . ." The food, provided by our own parish ladies, will include tasty Polish specialties and American favorites. Joe Szymzyck and his combo will contribute their talents and play a mix of traditional (plenty of polka tunes!) and contemporary. All who attended this event last year had a wonderful time and everyone is invited back.

JUST BETWEEN US

Summer's almost here, folks! As we all know, serving God is a year-round duty, and I'm sure we'll be seeing a full church each Sunday. Those early morning Masses are the perfect start when you're planning a day at the beach or a picnic in the park. Just as nature is in full bloom when the weather is warm, so should our souls be, and what better way to ensure this than to partici-pate in the holy sacrifice of the Mass. See you next week!

Yours in Christ,

Father Pat

Father Pat

SUFFER THE LITTLE CHILDREN

If you are a child, special guidelines for pre-Mass activities apply. First, wheedle change out of your mother for the collection basket. If she is foolish enough to give you her handbag to search through, dump its entire contents onto the pew in your impatience. In any event, after you have obtained the change, drop it on the floor at least once before Mass begins and lose it beneath the pew in front of you. Get down directly on the floor, behind the kneeler, reach under the next pew, brush the ankle of the lady sitting there, make her jump and start. Wait until her husband gruntingly reaches under his pew and retrieves the change, presenting it to you red-faced and out of breath. At this point your mother will reprimand you with flashing eyes and in a stage whisper for forgetting to use your special child's offering envelopes that were passed out in school.

Jostle your brothers and sisters for space and claim that they are hitting/pinching/bothering you, much as in the backseat of the car. Whine until you are separated and one of you is placed between your parents and another between your father and an old lady. Completely relax your spine and slither off the seat to protest this arrangement. Wince when your father firmly grasps your upper arm and hauls you back into an upright position. Begin to understand what the concept of temporal punishment for sin is all about.

What Every Catholic Lady Carries in Her Pocketbook

Personal missal
Laminated prayer cards
"Everyday" rosary beads
Emergency Kleenex
    (for headgear or child
    vomiting in church)
Offertory envelopes
Change for children's offering
Gloves
Several weeks' accumulation
    of church bulletins
Raffle ticket stubs
Mantillas (short and long,
    black and white)
Lifesavers to quiet fussy child
    during Mass
Lipstick, comb

"ALL PRAISE WE NOW OUR GOD"

Some of the most beautiful choral music ever written was intended to be sung during Mass. Historically it has been performed mainly by trained choirs, often made up of members of religious orders. Now, although there may still be a poorly rehearsed lay choir at Mass, all of the faithful are expected to raise their voices in song. The new repertoire reflects this: less Gregorian chant, more spirituals and what were formerly thought of as "Protestant" hymns; that is, music intended to be sung by amateurs.

As priest and entourage enter the church, the organ notes trill and swell. Please turn to the designated page of your hymnal or missalette and begin. . . .

"WITH HEART AND HANDS AND *VOICES*"

Lives there a Catholic, practicing or lapsed, whose heart (and conscience) does not leap at the melody of his favorite hymns? Of course, in fairness, one must admit that Catholic choirs are by and large dreadful. Lots of eager-

ness, lots of heart, but they will never compete in the same league with the Baptists or, God forbid, the Methodists.

Catholic churches for the most part now post the numbers of hymn selections on a board at the front, much as Protestant churches have traditionally done. Hymn aficionados can check out what's going to be sung ahead of time: if your favorites have been overlooked, choose another Mass!

Music lovers should take special note that many parts of the Mass proper are now being sung. Real enthusiasts might even consider the priesthood as an alternative career within the music field.

HYMN ETIQUETTE

Even if you can't carry a note in a bucket, you'll look grim, rebellious and plain sour if you don't at least mime the part. Pick up the hymnal (Jesus will love you all the more if you share it with the elderly contralto sitting next to you) and mouth the words. You'll feel stupid, but it must be done.

Try, every now and again, to join in on the refrain. Here's a simple one, with syllabification and accent marks:

"Iń-fi-innn-í-it thy vaást dó-o-maín; é-ver-lá-as-ting í-is thy reígn."

Soon, you will have a personal favorite. Herewith, a list of the top ten all-time Catholic "picks":

1. **"Ave Maria."** By a landslide. Chosen indiscriminately for weddings *and* funerals.
2. **"Holy, Holy, Holy."** A rousing, chorus-line type of song.
3. **"Tantum Ergo."** Good music, tricky lingo. "Tantum ergo makes your hair grow" sometimes mouthed by young girls. Venial sin, that.
4. **"Rock of Ages."** Not a Catholic hymn.
5. **"Kum-Ba-Ya."** Hymn of African origin, especially popular at folk Masses. Incorporates intricate hand motions.
6. **"Holy God We Praise Thy Name."** Standard fare; opens show.
7. **"Alleluia, Alleluia."** Easter song in which Jesus "bursts his prison bars."
8. **"Jesus Loves Me."** Again, not a Catholic hymn. "'Cause the Bible [dead Protestant giveaway] tells me so. . . ."
9. **"Adeste Fideles"** ("O Come All Ye Faithful" to post-Vatican II types). At Christmas, of course.
10. **"Amen."** Negro spiritual made famous in the movie *Lilies of the Field*. Again, often used at folk Masses; clapping featured.

THE MASS ORDINARY AND PROPER

Most of the Mass takes place within a prescribed and predictable format. Certain parts never change and are known as the ordinary. Others vary with each service and are called the proper. But from the Kyrie through the Gloria, the Collect, the Gradual, the Creed, the Offertory, the Lavabo, the Secrets, the Canon, the Our Father, Communion, the Ablutions, the Post-Communion Prayer and the Benediction, the faithful know pretty much what to expect.

There are a few notable exceptions. Different hymns are chosen for the beginning, Communion period, and end of each Mass, and the major scriptural readings—Introit, Epistle and Gospel—change each time also. But it is the sermon that is most personal and most specific to the occasion on which it is used, although certain themes seem to recur. The sermon is the one liturgical feature of a particular Mass that will most likely make you remember that service—or want to forget it.

PROCLAIM THE GOOD NEWS UNTO THE PEOPLE

Like a good after-dinner speech, a proper sermon begins with a joke, an amusing anecdote or a personal observation. "So the old priest says to the Mother Superior . . ."; "Just this morning Mrs. McMahon, the rectory housekeeper . . ."; "Bernadette, the parish station wagon, needed new spark plugs this week so . . ."

Ostensibly, the sermon bears some relation to the scriptural readings that precede it, particularly the Gospel. The sermon is the priest's opportunity to expand upon and interpret God's word for the laity. But to everything there is a season, the Bible tells us, and sermons are no exception.

THE FUND-RAISING SERMON/STATE OF THE PARISH MESSAGE

Akin to a family showdown on finances, this is when Father reports on the costs of parish upkeep for the previous year. The handymen of the parish have been generous with their time, the parish council has stretched every last penny, the ladies have supplied superb floral arrangements and felt appliqué banners for the altar, but a new plumbing system/ furnace/air-conditioner/carpet/organ/roof/car/rectory is needed, or, God forbid, a new church. This sermon is never pleasant for anyone, and a special coffee-and-pastry social hour often follows Mass that day. The scriptural passage about Jesus driving the moneylenders from the temple is never used in conjunction with this sermon.

THE MISSIONARY SERMON

Once or twice a year, a priest from a far-off, primarily non-Catholic, land arrives to explain how he and the colleagues he has left behind are saving souls and improving lives. He is generally of African, Asian or Irish origin. In any case, his accent is charming, if incomprehensible, and his priestly vestments are embroidered with colorful native designs. The collection plate is passed twice—first for the parish, then for the mission. The mission gets less than the parish, but that's okay—the mission priest will be making more North American appearances than The Who, delivering the same sermon each time, before he returns to his distant home.

THE POLITICAL-ISSUE SERMON

Extremely popular during the Vietnam years, especially at folk Masses. Favorite topic these days is nuclear disarmament. Generally delivered not more than a couple of times a year, and then only when the Bishop has written an official letter on the matter, or *Time* magazine has done a cover story, whichever comes first. More frequent than usual when priest is under thirty; priest has sideburns extending below mid-ear, or any other facial hair; church architecture is modern; in university communities (practically every other week!). *Never* at renegade Latin rite services.

FIRE-AND-BRIMSTONE SERMON

Though the Church has recently relaxed some of its more severe strictures, this sermon is still occasionally heard. It will *always* be heard when you bring non-Catholic friends to church, or when you go to Mass for the first time after a lengthy lapse in attendance. References to Hell, man's unworthiness, God's wrath, and X-rated movies are plentiful and vivid. A favorite of older priests, the fire-and-brimstone sermon often has dubious theological underpinnings. But if all it takes to make the old guy happy is convincing you that you might scrape the fender of your *mother's* car if you don't attend Mass on the Feast of the Assumption (when Jesus' Blessed *Mother* was taken up into Heaven), why not play along?

HOLIDAY SERMONS

Holiday sermons are generally brief and to the point. Energies have been drained and attention spans are short. Nevertheless, the occasion does not pass without due comment.

Christmas. Father deplores the commercialism of the holiday, urges everyone to drive safely on icy roads. See you real soon; unless Christmas falls on a Sunday, you are obligated to return for another Mass in less than a week. Optional: Father may mention that no one really knows the exact date or place of Jesus' birth.

Easter. Father scolds those who attend Mass only twice a year, taking seats from regular Massgoers. Thanks God for beautiful spring weather, or commiserates about rain which will spoil outdoor fun but bring families closer together.

Holy Days of Obligation. Father compliments those who populate the mostly empty pews, sighs over those who are not attending. That's it. Most communicants have worked all day before attending, and a lengthy sermon would invite general walkout directly following consecration.

LORD, I AM NOT WORTHY TO RECEIVE YOU

GOING UP

Those who desire to receive Holy Communion must ask themselves two important questions. First, Am I free from mortal sin? Second, How do I get in line, receive and return to my seat with a minimum of bother? The second question is not as simple as it seems, because most Communion lines resemble Los Angeles freeways. They are crowded, seem to run in all directions, and are full of people who are not really paying attention to what they are doing.

Some rather old-fashioned churches have retained the use of the Communion rail. To receive in such a case, simply follow the person in front of you, approach the rail, take the first available space on the kneeler and wait for the priest. You should be in prayerful contemplation at this time. You may, however, note the exceptional efficiency and teamwork (or lack thereof) with which priest and altar boy serve Communion. If the rail is a long one, the effect is especially dramatic. Sometimes, at a crowded Mass, two or more priests will each take a section of a very long rail, like so many power mowers working a large and overgrown lawn.

Many parishes now station the priest and one or more lay servers at various points throughout the church, making for quicker service and shorter but more chaotic Communion lines. In these more progressive churches, one generally takes Communion standing up, and has the choice of receiving the host directly on the tongue or in the hand, thence to be inserted in the mouth.

RECEIVING

The host can present practical problems. One variety, formerly standard, is pure white, paper thin and paper flavored. It is just about the size of a Necco wafer. This type of host has an unnerving tendency to stick to the roof of the mouth with a persistence unequaled even by creamy peanut butter

An Altar Boy's Prayer

LORD GOD MOST POWERFUL,
DELIVER US FROM THOSE EVILS
WHICH MAY BEFALL AN ALTAR
BOY.

From Hot Wax of Easter
Candles
DELIVER US, O LORD

From Cassocks Which Make
Us Trip
DELIVER US, O LORD

From Mixing up the Water
and the Wine
DELIVER US, O LORD

From Kneeling at the Wrong
Time
DELIVER US, O LORD

From Forgetfulness of Our
Responses
DELIVER US, O LORD

From Incense That Makes Us
Sneeze
DELIVER US, O LORD

From Serving Two Masses in
One Day
DELIVER US, O LORD

From Bridegrooms Who Tip
Cheaply
DELIVER US, O LORD

HOW TO AVOID INTERFAITH FAUX PAS
At Communion and Otherwise

When bringing non-Catholic friends to Mass, tell them to do everything you do. Otherwise, they won't know when to stand, sit or kneel. They'll look foolish and won't think much of you as a friend. Make sure, however, that they do not follow you up to receive Communion. They'll have to convert before that will be acceptable. You may already have them well on their way, but not yet.

When you visit a non-Catholic house of worship, simply sit quietly and observe. Anything more would compromise your religious principles. So what if you look foolish? Offer it up.

on white bread. You may attempt to pry the host loose with the tip of your tongue, or to suck it free. It is not considered seemly, however, to make too much of a display of this.

Do not chew the host. Remember that you are dealing with the Body of Christ, under the appearance of bread and/or wine. To chew the host would be an indignity. Forget what indignities the host will suffer when it hits the hydrochloric acid in your stomach. Forget that choking to death is an indignity also. Remember that the orders never to chew the host came from the same nuns who baked it. Which did they want more—to keep their handiwork intact until the last possible moment, or to give a good scare?

Some churches have begun to administer Communion "under both species"—bread *and* wine. This has made the consumption of the host easier, since the wine helps to wash it down. Also, in recent years slightly thicker, larger, whole-wheat or other hearty-grained hosts have replaced the very white, very thin "Wonder wafers" in many parishes. These newfangled hosts might present worse problems than the others, if the communicant tried to swallow one without chewing. Not to worry—in parishes progressive enough to use the new hosts, it is understood that they may be chewed.

DROPPING THE HOST
Whatever happens, try never to drop, spit out or otherwise bring insult or injury to the consecrated host. If you do, you may provoke a reaction almost as strong as if you had

yelled *"Fire!"* in a crowded theater. The altar boy or priest may throw his body upon the fallen host, and then consume it immediately himself. If the host falls upon a carpeted floor, the section of fabric surrounding it may have to be taken up and burned, since the material may contain tiny particles of the Body of Christ. At the very least, any visible pieces of the fallen host will be collected by the priest and placed in a sacred vessel for proper disposal later, and the floor will be scrubbed thoroughly. Dropping the host is somewhat like dropping a loaded tray in a school cafeteria. You will probably not be the butt of claps, jeers and gloating laughter, but you will receive looks of stern disapproval and pitying condescension. Be careful.

SEEK AND YE SHALL FIND
Getting Back to Your Seat After Communion

Proper devotional posture when returning to the pew after receiving Communion includes walking with hands folded and eyes slightly downcast. Do not look down so far or so continuously, however, that you lose track of where your seat is. If you walk just past your pew and realize this, it is acceptable to turn around calmly and make your way to your seat.

If you realize that you have miscalculated more than a little and cannot find your seat at all, continue walking all the way to the back of the church. Take all the time you need to survey the congregation, pick out some navigation points, then walk confidently and directly to your seat. If you maintain the proper devotional pace, very few people, if any, will notice. Above all, never panic, never look sharply about.

Once you have returned to your seat, kneel quietly for a few moments and fold your hands in prayer. If you are feeling very holy, you may actually place your face in your hands. Be sure to be aware of when everyone else has resumed a sitting or standing position, however, or again you may find yourself looking a bit silly.

CATHOLIC GESTURES
In addition to blessing yourself and genuflecting, there are a few other gestures that should be in every Catholic's repertoire. Several are useful

both during Mass and on other occasions.

1. Blessing your forehead, lips and heart when the Gospel is read at Mass. (Make a tiny Sign of the Cross at each spot with your thumbnail.)
2. Beating your breast during the Confiteor at Mass. Also known as *mea culpa*-ing.
3. Putting your face in your hands after Communion. For the truly pious.
4. Bowing your head when you say "Jesus." (Anytime.)
5. Folding your hands in prayer. (Anytime.)

A QUICK TAKE ON FASTING

Before receiving Holy Communion, a Catholic is required to fast for one hour, not taking any food or drink except water. Formerly pre-Communion fasting regulations were much stricter. Indeed, it was not uncommon to have a case or two of fainting at Mass, especially on holidays, hot summer days and at late-morning services. Usually the victim was a child or elderly person, making the incident all the more poignant, the self-denial all the more inspirational.

Fainting while actually in the Communion line (better

Fasting Time Line

Creation
Adam and Eve, the only human beings, are free to eat anything anytime, except the fruit of the Tree of Knowledge. No Catholic Church, no Communion, no fast.

↓

A.D. 1–1952
No water or food after midnight. Faucets tied shut in case children get up in middle of night in search of a drink.

↓

1952–1965
(Second Vatican Council ends) Water anytime. Otherwise, no food or drink for three hours before.*

↓

1965–
Current regulations as above.†

---

*Depending upon the degree of orthodoxy of your family, you might be able to take fruit juice, in moderate quantity, at any time before leaving the house, without being considered (by your parents, at least) to have broken the fast. In some Catholic households, however, the distinction between "water" and "liquids" became so blurred that the fast was violated by the pre-Mass consumption of copious amounts of Tiger's Milk, Carnation Instant Breakfast, Nestlé's Quik, Nutrament and the like.

†It is practically impossible not to observe the one-hour fast, what with travel time to church and then a good thirty-five minutes or so until Communion. Unless, of course, you take your breakfast with you, or gulp a handful of unconsecrated hosts sometimes sitting on a table just inside the portals of the church, waiting to be transferred by parishioners one by one into the chalice.

still: at the rail) was particularly dramatic and drew the attention of the congregation even faster than a parent scolding a naughty child. Fainting in the pews took on a more muffled aspect, and some people might not even learn about such an incident until after Mass was over.

For better or worse, the current fasting rules have put a stop to most fainting during Mass.

The time line (left) summarizes the changes from then to now.

MASS—THE BARE MINIMUM

How late can you arrive and still fulfill the obligation?

Just before the Gospel. (Generally about fifteen minutes into Mass.)

How early can you leave and still fulfill the obligation?

Following post-Communion prayers. (Generally about ten minutes before Mass ends.)

Please note that these little-publicized Church rules are not intended to encourage tardiness or skipping out early; both are frowned upon. Some rather lackadaisical Catholics try to stretch the Church's generous margin for error even farther. They arrive during the Gospel and leave just as the priest begins to serve Communion. In the view of strict Catholics, this is not the Mass of the Faithful— it is the Mass of the Heathen.

THE MASS IS ENDED, GO IN PEACE

It is over. You are free to leave. Well, Communion is over. You *can* leave without committing a mortal sin. And you do. Why? Because you are about to partake in one of the many traditional *après*-Mass activities, some of which have more to do with religious observance than others:

1. You want to get to the bakery before the rest of the church gets there.
2. You want to get the papers before the store runs out.
3. You are planning to race to the candy store to break your fast with M&Ms.
4. You have your bathing suit on under your Sunday clothes and your friends are parked outside waiting to go to the beach.

5. You've overslept and you're about to miss the beginning of the biggest football game of the season.

6. You are playing in a CYO basketball game and you have to go home and change first.

7. You are a public schooler who has to go to religious instruction but first you want to stop at your friend Jimmy's.

8. You want to be the first one out of the parking lot.

9. You have fulfilled the obligation and just want to go home and go back to bed.

Of course, not everyone dashes off the minute Mass is over. There are plenty of things to do around the church if you are so inclined.

IDLE HANDS ARE THE DEVIL'S PLAYTHINGS

Spare time on your hands? Whether your specialty is dusting pews or coaching basketball, you'll be put right to work if you donate hands, heart and soul to improving parish life. Seven days a week, from 7:00 A.M. to 7:00 P.M., whether you're seven or seventy, there's something for everyone. As a special bonus, indulgences of some indefinite but probably substantial amount are being earned all the while you grovel around in the name of your parish.

Even "fun" activities like singing in the choir will earn you points upstairs, but it's a generally known fact that the harder and more inconspicuously you work for your parish, the more good grace showers down. It's easy to see that the parish council president who pores over the parish finances at three in the morning will spend less time outside the pearly gates than the self-important "talking head" who jumps up to read the Epistle at Mass. Certainly God appreciates the people who fill the glamorous, show-biz jobs, but those parishioners might want to supplement their offering by ironing a few cassocks.

PARISH ACTIVITIES FOR YOU TO TRY

Babysitting during Mass
Teaching CCD classes
Driving shut-ins to Mass
Working at school cafeteria or library
Rolling quarters from collection baskets
Being an usher
Editing parish bulletin
Helping rectory housekeeper
Selling chances for parish raffle
Organizing after-Mass donut-and-coffee hours
Monitoring school playground
Shrouding statues at Lent
Serving on parish council

THE PARISH BAZAAR

KNOCK OVER THE MILK BOTTLE!

Many parishes hold an annual Fall Fest or Spring Fling in an effort to bring the parish family closer together and, more important, to bring in extra revenue.

The men of the parish construct a skeleton of wooden

THE GREAT BINGO SCANDAL

The vestibule of Holier Than Thou was abuzz after the ten o'clock Mass. From the pulpit, Father had confirmed the rumors that certain parish council members of neighboring St. Agatha's parish had indeed been indicted on seven counts of unlawful gambling. It seems the folks at St. Agatha's had taken Bingo a step further than the good Lord intended, and before the organizers could even make a good confession, they were locked away, humiliating themselves, their families and St. Agatha's. Church or not, the law's the law.

While a jackpot at Holier Than Thou's Bingo night could treat a family to a lavish hamburger dinner, a triumphant win at St. Agatha's would have the victor investigating tax-exempt bonds. Catholics and non-Catholics alike responded fervently to St. Agatha's massive "Win a Bundle" campaign and thousands of hopefuls crowded the parish hall every Wednesday night.

Then the shakedown. From the highway billboards touting to-be-won almighty dollars, to the leaflets mailed to wealthy speculators all over Wisconsin, some of St. Agatha's tactics were deemed a bit gamy by the officers of the law. The state officials did not look kindly on the dim lighting, the cafeteria ladies-cum-cigarette girls or on the ten-dollar minimum "donation" that slid across the green-felt-topped table in exchange for each Bingo card.

But the last nail on the cross was finding Sister Claire in the back room, methodically telephoning people who might want to know that Roy Sneed was having a lucky streak that night, inquiring if they would be interested in making a "donation" to the parish in his name.

The revelations shocked members of Holier Than Thou parish. Their own sparsely attended Bingo nights consist of the school cafeteria's long tables dotted with tin ashtrays full of popcorn-kernel markers. A tired jumble of senior citizens, nuns and young families, their arms filled with tiny parishioners, perch on folding chairs, anticipating. Up front, Ken Smith, the burly Knights of Columbus president, draws each numbered Ping-Pong ball carefully from its air-whipped Plexiglas box. "I-nineteen," he bellows into the squealing microphone, as the fiery plume on his K of C helmet sways precariously. "Bingo!" Margaret Morales ejaculates from the back of the cafeteria. So ends another staid but safe evening of Holier Than Thou Bingo.

Afterward, Ken Smith and Father McGillicuddy total the evening's meager profits, then smile broadly. Pulling out racing forms, they decide that St. Elmo's Fire is the horse to back and surreptitiously make a call to their bookie. It's all or nothing for Holier Than Thou.

booths that are garnished with bright banners announcing an imaginative array of games to be played and prizes to be won. Volunteers work each booth, quarters jingling in their tie-on apron pockets. The basket-'o'cheer drawing, cake walk, Sno-Cone booth, knock-over-the-milk-bottle game and fish pond all have their fans, but it is the success of the raffle that determines whether a new organ can be purchased this year.

A shiny new car, procured by a parish member "in the business," is the grand prize. Runners-up will be awarded toaster ovens, cameras or cookware sets. Each family in the parish has received a stack of raffle tickets to sell. Once the children have grown tired of hawking them to neighbors, the remainder are purchased by each family—unless the dog accidentally eats them first.

The parish bazaar is also an opportunity for the domestically oriented to show off their skills. So what if Mrs. Malloy's raisin cake goes down like a ton of bricks? So what if the thumbs of Mrs. Paribello's mittens are the size of small potatoes? You don't have to like it, but you're a member of the parish, and you're expected to buy something. At least the money's going for a good cause, it's tax deductible and you'll surely gain an indulgence or two.

THE CATHOLIC GETAWAY

For many of the faithful, the ideal vacation is one that combines sightseeing and pleasure with a religious experience, so that the soul as well as the body can be recharged. As they make their travel plans, the devout often consult the literature of tour operators not unlike Heavenly Haunts Pilgrimage Travel, Inc. Excerpts from Heavenly's latest brochure are presented in the hope that you, too, will want to "go with God."

A NOTE FROM THE TOUR DIRECTOR

I would like to thank you for taking the time to look over our latest Heavenly Haunts brochure. This year we are offering what we feel is our most outstanding and inspiring selection of tours ever. Whether you are planning a day in the country away from the hustle and bustle, a weekend jaunt, a full-scale vacation or a serene retreat, Heavenly Haunts offers a tour that is sure to appeal to your heart, soul and pocketbook.

Many people have the mistaken idea that a pilgrimage is "all pray and no play." I would like to take this opportunity to dispel this unfortunate notion. The aim of our tours is to relax you so that you can fully appreciate the beauty of God's creation. After all, "recreation" is just "creation" with a "re" in front of it. Here at Heavenly Haunts, we believe that a pilgrimage of the deepest religious significance can be combined with first-class social, cultural, sports, leisure and educational opportunities.

We at Heavenly Haunts feel particularly qualified to offer this type of tour, with more than fifty years of travel experience under our seatbelts. Our accommodations and land, sea and air carriers are among the most modern, efficient and luxurious available. (Camels in the Holy Land excluded, but that's all part of the fun!) Accompanied as you are by your very own group chaplain, you can rest assured that spiritual refreshment and solace will always be available, even in the unlikely event of an emergency.

Finally, I'd like to note that because of the continuing patronage of our many veteran travelers, and all the new "converts" they've recruited, our prices are in every case the same or lower than last year's.

And now a word from Heavenly Haunts' spiritual adviser, Father Lawrence "Reds" Shenanigans.

Julia P. Costello

Julia P. Costello
Tour Director

Once again I'm delighted to be serving as Heavenly Haunts' spiritual adviser and to be working with Heavenly's fine and able staff, headed by the lovely Julia Costello. (Hope to see you in Capri again this year, Julia.) I can only concur heartily that a pilgrimage is an opportunity to refresh the body and mind as well as the soul; an occasion for fun and laughter as well as piety.

Nevertheless, it is important to keep in mind that prayer and penance are the essential ingredients of any pilgrimage. God is everywhere, but He seems to favor certain beautiful "Heavenly Haunts" here on His Earth. If you are interested solely in sightseeing and indulging the flesh, perhaps Club Med would be more to your liking. But if what you are looking for is a wholesome, stimulating, enjoyable but above all pious and spiritually energizing journey, then welcome aboard!

Yours in Christ,

Fr. Larry "Reds" Shenanigans

Father Lawrence Shenanigans

THE CAPE CODDER
5 Days—$589.00
(Includes three meals of your choice, offerings for the collection basket at St. Francis Xavier.)
Leave Sept. 12, 5:00 A.M.
Return Sept. 16

A restful five days of touring and sailing in the Cape Cod area. Mass is offered each morning at St. Francis Xavier Church in Hyannis, where the Kennedy family worships. There'll be an afternoon of boating near Hyannis Port, and day sails to Martha's Vineyard, Provincetown and Newport. Dinner is available each night at any of the beautiful Hyannis restaurants where the Kennedy family eats. To help us recover our "land legs," the last day will feature a motor excursion (by deluxe coach) to the Warwick Malls in Rhode Island and Our Lady of La Salette Shrine in North Attleboro, Massachusetts.

Bring topsiders and cameras. Tour not given during America's Cup years.

THE BAWDY
4 Days—$5,850.00
(Includes complimentary choice of ales, biscuits and cold meat pies whenever desired; handling of one tankard or knapsack.)
Leave May 1, 9:00 A.M.
Return May 4

Merrye Olde England was not so merrye for several of our Catholic martyrs. On our three-day English pilgrimage by foot—ideal for the pious, "well-heeled" weekender—we will re-live many of the scenes from Chaucer's *Canterbury Tales*—bedding down in the hay by the side of a genuine country lane included. Beginning at London's Heathrow Airport, where we cheerfully decline a lift on the shuttle bus, we wind up full of good food and drink at the cathedral site of the martyrdom of Thomas à Beckett (known to filmgoers as one of Richard Burton's best roles). After an hour's rest we will be marching "double time" back to London and the infamous Tower site of the martyrdom of Mary Queen of Scots. Then it's a mad dash over to Heathrow again—here's where you joggers and marathon runners will have a real advantage. Spanning the centuries in an instant, we board our British Airways Concorde to zip back to the States across the pond. Good show!

Passport, proof of bubonic plague inoculation and a note from your cardiologist are required. Cheerio.

THE SIX-PACKER
3 Full Days—$598.00
(Includes free border passage, six-pack of Canadian beer of your choice, two meals, handling of one piece of luggage.)
Leave Jan. 5, 7:30 A.M.
Return Jan. 7.
Expect to be back in the land of the free and the brave no later than 8:00 P.M.

Visit Quebec, the historic "Land of Miracles" in the "Great White North." We'll start with a stop at Cap de la Madeleine, the Canadian national shrine to Our Lady. There will be plenty of time in the afternoon for a stroll, contemplative prayer or browsing in the well-stocked gift shop. The morning of the second day will be spent in prayerful contemplation, while in the afternoon we visit Martyr Country, including a moment of silence at the Shrine of Our Lady of the Tomahawk. We come to the highlight of our trip on the third day, when we will witness a miracle at historic St. Anne de Beaupré. (For more details, check your program the day of the miracle.) We return home later that day, exhausted but enriched.

Bring proof of American citizenship.

THE HOLY, HOLY, HOLY: FOR THE TRULY DEVOUT
40 Days and 40 Nights— $40,000
Leave Ash Wednesday
Return Palm Sunday
All inclusive

This very special tour is for the sack cloth and ashes crowd, for those who wish to visit the chief shrines of Europe and the Holy Land while avoiding worldly temptation. We begin in Ireland at Knock, site of one of Our Lady's documented visitations. There you will be introduced to a monk of your choice, who will be your constant companion during the next forty days and nights. From Knock we travel to London, where we will restrict our five-day itinerary to the insides of the great churches and cathedrals. Your monk will blindfold you when transportation is called for. Then it's a full week in Lourdes, and five days each in Paris and Rome. Itinerary for the great capital cities: as in London. For one breathtaking day we'll witness the Passion Play at Oberammergau. Finally it's on to the Holy Land for an extended two-week stay, during which you will visit every site of religious or historical interest you've ever heard of, and many you haven't. Too numerous to mention here, the highlights include the Chapel of Flagellation, Golgotha and the Via Dolorosa. There will be plenty of time each and every evening of the tour for spiritual exercises with your monk. Since we'll be staying in monasteries all along the way, and fasting often, this tour remains a superb value as well as the most pious of pilgrimages.

Just bring your passport and you.

ITEMS FROM *HIS* CATALOG

Priests, nuns and parish councils shop from catalogs just like the rest of us. They can buy vestments, habits, chalices, church decorations and the like. Here are some items which might prove more useful in the daily life of most parishes.

Choir Snuffer. Attention choir directors! Ever wanted to tone down that one off-key singer without interrupting the hymn? The Choir Snuffer is the answer to your prayers! Introduced just a few years ago, this ingenious device has quickly become one of our most popular items. The design derives from the traditional candle lighter/extinguisher, and now lends itself to an entirely new function, all in keeping with the increasing role of amateur parish choirs in the liturgy. Comes with its own upright holder. Stands at the right hand of the choir director and is light enough to be operated easily with one arm while director continues to conduct with the other. Here's how it works: Unique "double-acting" hood is lowered over head of offending songster, preventing him from following the music and deafening him with the sound of his own discordant voice at the same time. 100 percent money-back guarantee.

Hair-Shirt Scapular Vests. Created by the Sisters of the Holy Veil in Omaha, these itchy wonders are painstakingly woven of locks shorn from the Sisters' own heads. Designed for folks wanting to do their penance on Earth, the vests are guaranteed to get rougher and more irritating with wear. Ideal for that martyr-to-be on your gift list.

"To-the-Last-Note" Automatic Door Guards. Annoyed by parishioners leaving just as singing of recessional hymn begins, or even at Communion? Install these handsome "choir screen" grill-work door guards! Ensure rousing final choruses and generous offerings at the third collection! Automatically opens after last organ note is played, or if smoke detector is activated.

Lobster-Trap Collection Basket. Easy to drop money in, but impossible for greedy fingers to "make change." Brings a touch of New England charm to any parish.

Priest and Nun Halloween Costumes. Sized for toddlers to teens, authentic costumes are popular with parents who wish to inspire children to religious vocation at an early age. Girls pick traditional Sisters of the Holy Ghost or whimsical *Flying Nun* headdresses. Flowing gown, crucifix necklace and from-the-waist rosary beads included with each ensemble. Boys choose black button-down Jesuit cassock with matching rope cincture, or colorful High Mass set complete with alb, gaily decorated chasuble and stole. True to every detail, costumes also make fine outfits for midget priests and nuns.

California-Style Baptismal Font. Designed for en masse Baptisms, this handsome redwood tub washes away Original Sins of up to four swinging converts. Doubles as after-hours Jacuzzi for parish priests.

"Scent-Around" Automatic Incense Dispenser. Say good-bye to messy, dangerous censers and time-consuming processions. Our unique incense-dispensing system utilizes strategically placed wall outlets throughout church to release scents quickly, evenly and safely—all at the touch of a button behind the altar. Carbon dioxide "fog" and colored smoke may also be dispensed and combined with phased lighting for stunning special effects. Standard aromas plus special "scents of the season" packages are available—Christmas Evergreen, Burnt Palm for Ash Wednesday, Easter Lilies.

Rosary Tape Cassette. "Say" the Rosary without saying a word. Slip the tape into your Walkman before your early morning run and jog with God.

Altar Auto-Wash. Put an end to the drudgery of washing the chalice and other eucharistic vessels by hand. Free your parish priest to spend more "quality" time with congregation during Mass. Can be installed permanently in back of altar, or works equally well as portable model for mission, chapel or other temporary site. Unique "rinse-hold" cycle for large active parishes with many Sunday morning Masses. Never again will you hear a child say, "Mommy, can we go home after the priest finishes washing the dishes?"

Comes in white, avocado, copper. Interchangeable front panels in liturgical colors available. Three water settings—hot, cold, holy. Safe for most Communion ware.

TGIF Dining-Room Spray. A handy aerosol spray that permeates the room with the odor of fish. A favorite of old-timers who may now consume meat on Fridays, yet remember fondly the fishy smell that lingered in their homes the Fridays of yesteryear. Available in your choice of tuna casserole or Mrs. Paul's fragrances.

Priest's Reversible Coat. Attractive, well-made coat designed to give double service. One side traditional black, in a practical polyester/cotton blend, perfect over our rabats or clerical shirts. Reverses to a cool, comfortable 100 percent Indian madras plaid in nonbleeding colors. Just right for the priest on the go who dashes incognito from church to singles' bars searching out the sinful.

Organ Dust Cover. Protect that costly parish organ! After each use, spread on this long-wearing slipcover. Clear plastic lets the organ's beauty shine through. Cover is embellished with lines from best-loved hymns, or, for a hip, with-it look, a selection of "graffiti-style" religious slogans in a rainbow of spray-paint colors. Doubles as attractive wall hanging. One size fits most organs.

Jolly Priest Tie-On Tummy. For the scrawny priest requiring an affable, fatherly image to win over his parishioners. Simply tie on this lightweight "tummy" under your alb, and folks will flock to you for sage counsel and congenial after-Mass bantering. Made of machine-washable Hollofil® in nonslip 100 percent cotton shell.

Dear Abbey:

I am a priest who recently moved into a new parish. The pastor called me aside shortly after I arrived to point out to me that my posture after Mass left something to be desired. When I asked him for a further explanation, he simply stated that talking to parishioners with my arms akimbo is not proper. What is the proper way to stand when talking to parishioners?—**Slouching Toward Bethlehem**

Dear Slouching:

The accepted manner of standing while talking to parishioners has always been with hands folded one over the other directly in front of the body, feet just slightly pointed outward at 45 degree angles from the body. Gently rocking onto the heels is acceptable if not done too rapidly. When speaking to female parishioners a slightly inclined posture is permitted but laughter should be confined to gentle chuckles. Slight waves of the hand and nods should be sprinkled throughout the period immediately following Mass. When moving from one parishioner to another, a slight touch of the hand on the arm and a "Bless you" should suffice to let them know that your conversation has drawn to a close.

Dear Abbey:

Sister Anne of our parish recently offered me a ride to our church bake sale, as the convent is just next door to us. However, Sister Anne, bless her heart, is one of the worst drivers I have ever encountered. It terrifies me to drive with her. She never exceeds 25 mph and indicates her turns so far in advance that cars following assume she must have a short in her taillights. We have had many near misses with the dear Sister driving. How do I decline a ride without hurting her feelings?—**Uneasy Rider**

Dear Uneasy:

Come on now. Recent insurance industry records show that nuns are responsible for fewer than .001 percent of all accidents on our highways. This is due in large part to the special attention Our Lord pays to His nuns. You are safer in a car with Sister A. than you are in the shower.

Dear Abbey:

I love to attend Mass on a daily basis, but I am becoming more and more uncomfortable when the time for the Sign of Peace approaches. There doesn't seem to be any rhyme or reason to how it is done. Some people kiss, some shake hands, some even stop to chat for a moment. It is impossible to tell who may be acquainted and who may be total strangers. The other morning I was particularly taken aback when three members of a family actually crossed the center aisle to greet others in the church. What is the proper Sign of Peace?—**Shaky**

Dear Shaky:

Despite what some may think, this is not a case of when in Rome do as the Romans do. The proper Sign of Peace is a firm, short handshake given while intoning "Peace be with you." A slight smile is fine in addition. Greet only those immediately to the front, sides and rear. The Sign of Peace should be like a familial kiss, short and sweet. It is not the time to compare golf scores or to find out which school So-and-So will be attending in the fall. It is permissible to exchange the Sign of Peace with those priests who leave the altar to join in, but only when you have an aisle seat. In my travels I have seen too many variations which left the church looking like a cocktail party in its late stages.

Dear Abbey:

I'm ten and my mom and dad are always inviting Father Joe over for dinner ever since he came to bless the house. I gotta get dressed up and keep a napkin on my lap all the way through dinner. I can't feed the dog under the table and they always talk about my schoolwork. I like Father Joe but why does he have to eat over at our house all the time?—**Fed Up**

Dear Fed:

When you grow older you will understand what an honor it is to have a priest eat dinner at your house. It establishes your family as one of the pillars of the parish and this stand-ing increases with each meal a priest has at your home. God keeps track of where priests eat. You should be happy that God is watching Father eat with you rather than Ronald Mc-Donald. P.S.: Never call a priest by his first name, even when he invites you to do so.

CATHOLIC FUN FACTS
The Numbers Game

DID YOU KNOW THAT . . .*

- There are 900,525,399 Catholics in the world besides you?
- The population of the U.S. is 22.7% Catholic?
- There are 219,369 parishes around the world?
- There are 819,279 Sisters but only 58,210 Brothers?
- The largest order of priests is the Jesuits with 21,955 members?
- The smallest order of priests is the Servants of the Holy Paraclete with thirty-two members?
- The leading states for Catholic colleges are New York and Pennsylvania?
- There have been 264 Popes?
- There are 154 Cardinals and 889 Bishops in the world?
- Ninety percent of all those who have claimed to possess the stigmata have been women?
- Twenty-three saints were canonized in the 1990s?
- The Pope's web address is www.vatican.va?

*Source: *The 2000 Catholic Almanac.*

IV

One, Holy, Catholic and Apostolic Church

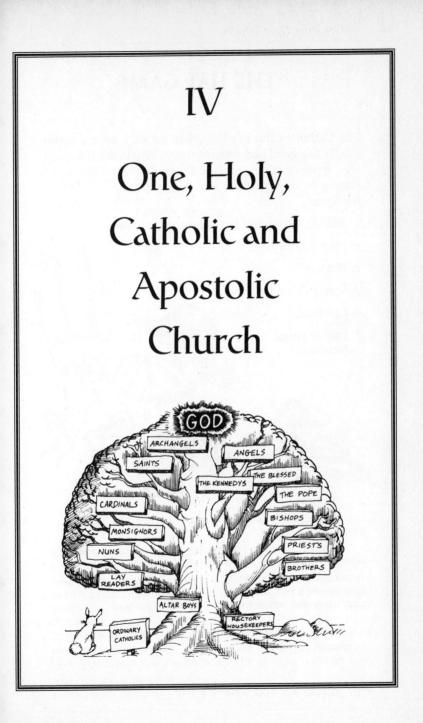

THE HAT GAME

The Catholic Church's hat creations for men are whimsically designed and proudly worn. What with the extensive array of styles, each with its own significance, it's simple to detect who's who solely on the basis of his headgear.

Match the person to his appropriate hat:

1. Pope (everyday)

2. Bishop

3. Usher at your parish

4. Cardinal

5. Father Guido Sarducci

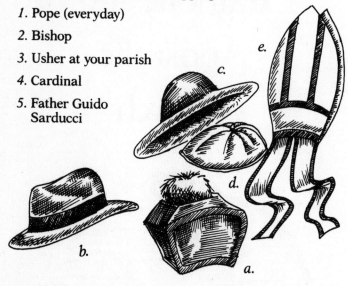

KEY:

1—*d.* Not a yarmulke, not a beanie, this is a calotte. Nice covering for a thinning crown.

2—*e.* The miter, also known as a tiara, is worn over the forehead in front. The flaps hanging down are called infulae.

3—*b.* This is a regular old fedora. It comes in a variety of dull shades.

4—*a.* The cardinal's biretta is a square red cap with three or four projections rising above the crown and a jaunty pompom on top. Bishops can wear birettas, too, in purple only.

5—*c.* The shovel hat, popularized by actor Don Novello's portrayal of Father Guido Sarducci.

RELIGIOUS FASHION

Aspiring nuns have a wide assortment of orders to choose from, each, like nursing schools, with their individual style of cap. Some imprudent orders have subscribed to an "anything goes" philosophy of dress. But what's the point of being a nun if you blend right in with all the other antinuke demon-

strators? You want reverence. You want respect. A classy uniform is key.

If you're in the market, investigate the garb before finding out anything else about an order. Does it flatter your shape and is it consistent with your own sensibilities of dress? No? Then on to another order. After all, you will be wearing the

FORCE OF HABIT

"The Traditional"   "The Sister Bertrille"   "The Thoroughly Modern" same outfit every day for the rest of your life. It pays to shop around.

A plump aspirant would do well to consider those flowing skirts popular with many orders. They flatter all figures and hide all sins while affording free and easy movement so important to the nun on the run. Rosary beads hanging from the waist help elongate the portly figure, although large, bulky rosaries tend to dwarf a tiny nun, no matter her girth. To grace a round face, look for a long veil to stretch out the features, and keep in mind that a tight wimple around the neck only accentuates a double chin. If you are troubled by sagging jowls, a headpiece that sweeps upward is the remedy. Remember *The Flying Nun?* That's the look for you.

BROTHERS

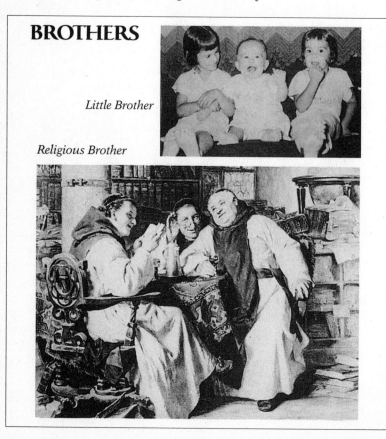

Little Brother

Religious Brother

Black, although a bit gloomy, is a "power color"; hence its popularity among the teaching orders. It's also quite slimming. If a cool white uniform appeals, investigate the nursing orders. Light-colored outfits especially become trim nuns who can nicely carry off a stylish cummerbund-type sash at the waist too.

No matter what your figure type or fashion flair, there's a religious order perfect for you. If you need help deciding, ask a nun whose judgment you trust.

WHAT EVER HAPPENED TO FATHER BROWN?
Profiles of Failed Priests

1.
FATHER DOMINICK

As a young priest in a small parish in New Jersey (St. Francis of the Bleeding Heart) in the early sixties, Father Dominick instituted guitar Masses. He countered the protests of the elderly parishioners, claiming that he was merely attempting to bring the young back to the Church by holding one folk Mass a week at midnight on Saturdays.

Despite the folk Masses and other innovations (field trips to rock concerts, etc.), there continued to be an erosion in the numbers of young Catholics in the parish. Father Dominick was gravely concerned and asked a recent graduate of the parish school why the young were disaffected. He was informed that there was a revolution going on in the streets and the

Church just wasn't where it's at.

In an attempt to get a handle on what was happening, Father Dominick accepted an invitation to an antiwar rally and rock concert. Toward the end of the rally, the police arrived and began making random arrests. Father intervened and yelled to the police, "Let my children go!" He received twenty stitches and was permanently radicalized. After several years of activism and several more in jail, convicted of pouring blood on draft records, Father left the priesthood.

He is currently tending bar in Hoboken at the Sign of the Cross Disco, of which he is part owner. He is married to former SDS organizer Margaret Dane. They have two children.

2.
FATHER MICHAEL AND SISTER MARY FATIMA

Father Michael was the dynamic young principal of Immaculate Conception High School in suburban Milwaukee. He was strict but kind, and well thought of by the students. Sister Mary Fatima, S.S.N.D., assistant principal and art teacher, was a chubby, friendly nun given to easy laughter and always willing to listen to a student's problems.

Together they presided over Immaculate Conception, instilling the virtues of hard work, fair play, love of country and strict adherence to Catholic doctrine. Many times they would work late into the night outlining lesson plans and arranging school functions.

One day in 1973, Father Michael and Sister Mary Fatima disappeared.

During the final dance of the school year, there appeared on the floor an adult couple no one seemed to know. The man was dressed in a silk print shirt and bright plaid pants. The woman wore a short white skirt and white plastic go-go boots. The astonished students soon realized they were Father Michael and Sister Mary Fatima.

Father Michael now has his real-estate license and sells in southern California. Sister Mary is a homemaker, throws pottery and is busy raising their two children.

3.
FATHER JIM ALEXANDER

Father Jim was the director of communications at a large midwestern Catholic university. He was also faculty adviser for the college radio station and drama department.

A frustrated actor, he would cast himself in the student plays as well as direct them. The local papers gave the college productions rave reviews and frequently commented on Father Jim's acting ability.

While attending a conference on media in New York last year, Father Jim was taking a stroll through the theater district. He loved the hustle of the crowd, the marquees announcing the latest hit shows and felt strangely attracted to it all. As he stood in front of the Winter Garden Theater, a short bald man in an expensive suit approached him shouting, "Perfect! You are just perfect!"

Father Jim is now best known as Rod Rockwell and can be seen Monday through Friday on the daytime drama *Last Life to Live* in the character of Dr. Frank Carter. He is still single though no longer associated with the Church.

NUN OF THE ABOVE

Sometimes nuns quit the convent for one reason or another, and, in taking up the lay life, continue to bear the indelible marks of the nunnery. Although some ex-nuns manage to leave behind the trappings completely, a larger percentage tend to retain certain sisterly traits.

An observant Catholic can generally spot an ex-nun with ease. Here's what to look for:

1. Impeccable posture
2. Well-groomed fingernails
3. Tasteful, low-key makeup
4. A serene smile
5. A penchant for navy blue outfits
6. Low-heeled shoes

Be aware that what appears to be an ex-nun may instead be a real nun in ex-nun's clothing. With relaxed dress restrictions in many orders, the distinction is almost academic.

HOW TO ENCOURAGE RELIGIOUS VOCATIONS

The Church has conceded that traditional strategies for encouraging vocations have not been successful. Church deacons—laypeople trained to take positions of special responsibility in parish life—will soon be eligible to perform all priestly functions except marriages and funerals. In order to avert the shock that this will undoubtedly produce in Catholics brought up with "that old-time religion," we suggest that a last-ditch effort be made to recruit additional religious personnel. Even if just one young man or woman is persuaded to take up the religious life, the following measures will have been worthwhile.

1. Don't call it celibacy; call it asexuality.
2. Don't keep priests and nuns tied to traditional roles. Allow them a full range of professional expression—as auto mechanics, architects, astronauts (a natural, all the closer to God!), etc.
3. Hire a "name"—Halston, Adolfo, Kenzo—to design clerical garb. Also, establish a line of religious cosmetics for nuns—Sacramental Siena eyeliner, Holy Grape lip gloss, Blessed Mother Blue eye shadow, Burnt Lenten Ash Blond hair coloring, Cardinal Red blush, Original Sin perfume.
4. Let the vows of poverty go by the boards. **Provide** clerics with sporty, late-model cars. They'll be happier and more effective spiritual counselors to today's upwardly mobile Catholics because of it.
5. Don't call them convents; call them condos.
6. Banish rectory housekeepers from the kitchen—engage *nouvelle cuisine* chefs instead.
7. Build retirement communities for the religious in Florida, not New Jersey, Ohio, North Dakota. Special features should include Betamax with tapes of Popes celebrating Christmas Mass, from John XXIII to whomever. Pick your favorite and celebrate with *Il Papa* again and again.

MIRACLES

Miracles have always played a major role in the Catholic faith, from the loaves and fishes to Fatima to the modern-day miracle of Ramona Barreras of Phoenix, Arizona: "When the tiny woman looked down and saw the face of Jesus in a tortilla . . ."

Here's a definitive way to tell if these far-out occurrences are fact or fantasy:

YOU KNOW IT WAS A MIRACLE IF . . .

- It happened to children. (It never happens to an older person.)
- It happened in some remote village in a foreign

country that nobody ever heard of. (It never happens in New York City.)

- They make a movie about it. (The things they write newspaper articles about are generally not miracles.)
- Mary or a saint or God makes a prediction about something. (Sometimes only the person who sees the miracle knows what the prediction is and you just have to trust that it came true.)
- Mary or a saint or God asks you to do something you don't want to do. (This happens almost every time.)
- Years after the miracle happened you get cured of something by going to the place where it happened. (You leave your cane or crutches lying around for other people to see.)
- They build a church where it happened. (Usually a *big* church.)
- Whoever sees the miracle grows up to be a priest or a nun. (They never end up driving a truck or herding sheep.)

THE STIGMATA

The most fascinating miracle to Catholic schoolchildren and grown-ups alike is the stigmata. These are the wounds of Jesus Christ (holes in the hands, feet and side) reproduced on a living devout Catholic. There have been about three hundred reported cases of the stigmata and although none is officially recognized by the Church, those belonging to St. Francis of Assisi are thought to be the most authentic.

To date there has been no scientific testing of a bearer of the stigmata, though one can easily imagine scientists the world over eager to conduct tests such as those done on the shroud of Turin and Uri Geller. Yet no one has come forward for such testing. But would it really prove

When Mother Mary Comes to Visit

The Blessed Virgin has had a fairly limited itinerary for her visits to Earth. In the following list of places Mary has graced with her presence, you will see some countries repeated:

1. Banneux, Belgium
2. Beauvaign, Belgium
3. La Salette, France
4. Lourdes, France
5. Knock, Ireland
6. Guadalupe, Mexico
7. Fatima, Portugal

anything if the scientific community had its field-testing day? What would they make of the "invisible" stigmata, which are reported to be just as painful for those who have them as the visible ones?

Maureen Kelly   April 21, 1969
Religion   6'

a miracles
b nature
c life and death
d faith
e suffering
f tax collector
g Heaven
h Paul
i twelve
j prophets

2 a paralyzed man could walk
b a dead girl raised to life
c two blind men could see
d a dumb man could hear
e a woman was cured from hemorrhage

RELICS

A relic is an object associated with a saint or martyr and revered for that reason. It might be part of the actual physical remains of a saint—a bone, for example. Or it could be something that was once owned, worn, touched or blessed by the holy personage.

To give a modern-day example, if Mick Jagger were to tear off his shirt at a Rolling Stones concert and throw it into the audience that shirt would be a relic of Mick Jagger. More particularly, it would be a relic of the miracle of Mick Jagger earning a fortune while performing the same old act. Would the shirt you were wearing at the concert be a relic of the concert as well? Probably not; more accurately, it would be called a memento or souvenir.

Catholic altars traditionally contain one or more relics of saints, as do Cardinals' rings, which is why you kiss them. Granted, there are an awful lot of saints. And at times it may seem to the ordinary Catholic that there are enough finger bones of saints for every man, woman and child in modern-day China. But do you think most relics are more on the order of Mick Jagger's shirt or the shirt you wore at a Rolling Stones concert?

THE SACRAMENTALS

Sacramentals are holy things or actions that call to mind God, the saints and spiritual truths. They include blessings given by priests and Bishops, exorcisms and special ceremonies such as Benediction and the Stations of the Cross. Most Catholics, however, think first of holy water, holy candles, ashes, palms, crucifixes, medals, rosaries, scapulars and images of Jesus, Mary and the saints when they think sacramental.

Unlike the sacraments, the sacramentals do not obtain God's grace for us directly, but only through the devotion they inspire in us. They are not to be thought of as objects of superstition or as good-luck charms. Remember this the next time you pick up a can of Miraculous Mother of Perpetual Help Deodorant Room Spray.

HOLY DAYS OF OBLIGATION

The Pope almost made many of the Holy Days of Obligation optional (doctrinal flip-flop), but at the last minute decided that an obligation is an obligation, not an option (doctrinal flip-flop-flip). Here is a list of those pesky days when you absolutely must attend Mass, even if they fall on a weekday:

Christmas Day *(December 25).* Christ was born.

Solemnity of Mary, Mother of God *(January 1).* Christ was circumcised.

Ascension Thursday *(Forty days after Easter).* Christ went to Heaven.

The Assumption *(August 15).* Mary disappeared and everyone assumed she went to Heaven.

All Saints' Day *(November 1).* A day to honor all the saints in Heaven and on Earth, known and unknown.

Immaculate Conception *(December 8).* This is the day Mary was conceived without Original Sin. It is *not* the day Christ was conceived. You are confusing it with the Virgin Birth.

Feasts of Saints Peter and Paul*

Feast of Corpus Christi*

St. Joseph's Day*

Feast of the Epiphany*

*We hope that these are Holy Days only in other countries, because sixty-two million American Catholics do not necessarily go to Mass on these days.

THE HOLIDAYS

Catholics are fond of holidays because just about all of them have religious underpinnings. Halloween, more than goblins and spooks, is the eve of All Souls' Day, and even on secular holidays like Thanksgiving and Veterans' Day, heads are bowed in prayer. Fervent Catholics call February 14 Saint Valentine's Day and like to check their Church calendar for offbeat saints' days to celebrate. But it is the Easter and Christmas seasons, resplendent with baubles, bangles and rosary beads, when all Catholics really shine. Whether on holiday, holy day or any other day of the year, Catholics help keep alive the saying "The family that prays together, stays together."

EASTER

Ash Wednesday marks the first day of Lent, the 40 days (or 960 hours) preceding Easter, when Catholics remember the sacrifice Jesus made when he spent 40 days fasting in the desert. Catholics today fast, too, though not as stringently as Our Lord did. In addition, they traditionally make a special sacrifice to atone for how sinful they have been the other 325 days of the year. On Ash Wednesday the faithful attend Mass, where holy ashes are daubed on their foreheads as the priest intones, "Thou art dust and unto dust thou shalt return." Enthusiastic children "freshen" their ashes during the day with cigarette ash.

Easter is the most joyous holiday in the liturgical calendar, as well it should be. Catholics who have managed to survive the fasting, Lenten sacrifice and the Easter duty

obligation of going to Confession during Lent deserve a little gaiety. Young devotees have been known to celebrate with a sort of wild abandon, when vast quantities of marshmallow chicks, cream-filled eggs and chocolate bunnies are consumed and a frenzied "chocolate high" ensues.

But before the festivities, it is necessary to participate in the day-by-day Holy Week services. The pre-Easter week begins on Palm Sunday, when branches of palm are brought home from church and placed behind crucifixes and holy pictures in the hallway, kitchen and bedrooms. According to Church regulation, last year's palms are taken down and burned, often in the backyard barbecue pit. Some families construct small crosses from extra palms, which are worn on a lapel or school uniform throughout the week.

Slowly Holy Week passes. More prayers than usual are said and Stations of the Cross become almost ritual. As they eat dinner on Holy Thursday, Catholics are reminded of the Last Supper, and they wonder if Jesus and the Apostles had also enjoyed a dinner of roast beef and mashed potatoes. They may also be curious about why Jesus had everyone sit on the same side of the table. Good Friday is invariably bleak and rainy, which hardly matters to young Catholics, since they are usually indoors observing a strict quiet time during the hours when Jesus hung on the cross. If they do slip out-side to play, observers will see but not hear them, as the devout youngsters go silently about their softball game.

By Easter Sunday, good Catholics have earned their jelly beans. Before feasting on lamb with mint jelly, families troop off to Easter Mass. There they take the opportunity to show off their

---

Giving Up

In parochial school classrooms the world over, children with smudged foreheads stand up one by one and announce their Lenten promises to teachers and classmates. There are boys in the back row who giggle that they will be giving up doing homework or going to Mass. The humor escapes Sister, who yells "Bold as brass!," and waves her ruler and marches down the aisle toward the offenders. She strides at such a ferocious pace that her veil flutters out behind her, prompting students on either side to crane their necks as she passes by. They hope to discover, once and for all, if nuns really do have hair.

Lenten pledges like "I'm going to work harder on my catechism," or "I will say extra prayers for the poor souls in Purgatory" are a little lame, but are nonetheless safe choices if you don't think you can give up anything for forty days. Besides, no one can tell if and when you slip

up. If you do give up something, say chocolate, it's crucial to keep with it for at least a couple of weeks. If you quit any sooner, you'll feel lousy and friends will snub you when you unwrap a candy bar at lunchtime. And don't try to sneak it. You'll feel even worse knowing God is the only one who knows.

By far the most risky Lenten offering is a promise to do something every day. Whether it is visiting the sick old lady down the street after school, or attending 7:00 A.M. Mass, a daily commitment is tough to endure, but tougher not to. "How are you doing?" Sister will cheerfully inquire, often at the precise moment you're considering throwing in the holy towel. "Fine, 'ster," you'll mutter, counting off the remaining days of Lent on your fingers. If you can manage to be vigilant in your daily duty until Easter, you will almost be able to feel that halo resting on your head.

Easter finery, which ranges from better-than-Sunday-best Robert Hall suits for boys to new dresses and maybe even gloves for the girls. Fathers look the way fathers always look on Sundays, though mothers may sport new flowery concoctions on their heads. Children prefer outfits designed with plenty of pockets so that they can easily tote a few goodies to slyly pop into their mouths after Communion.

CHRISTMAS

Christmas means different things to different people. For Catholics it's a time to flaunt their religion shamelessly, and abhor the commercialism of the season with even more gusto than non-Catholic neighbors. None of those glittery Advent calendars will do. Catholics especially avoid the Protestant types that make one feel like a contestant on *Let's Make a Deal* when the little door is opened each day. Instead Dad and the kids cover a Frisbee-sized Styrofoam ring with pine branches and insert one pink and three purple candles to signify the four weeks of Advent. As Christmas approaches, one new candle is ceremoniously lit each Sunday night and everyone argues about whose turn it is to light it. Catholic families with more than four children often opt for two or even three wreaths per season.

Setting up the nativity scene is a traditional pre-Christmas ritual. Each figure, whether cast in crystal by Waterford glassblowers or in colorful plastic by Koreans, is unwrapped and placed lovingly in the stable. Children adore this seasonal dollhouse and often invent novel plights for the odd cast of characters; for example, Mary balanced on the hump of a camel.

The nuns at Holier Than Thou inspire their own holiday traditions, encouraging their charges to bring in lots of canned goods "so that poor children will have as nice a Christmas as you." In addition, the Sisters send every child home with folders of Holy Childhood Christmas seals to peddle to unsuspecting relatives and neighbors. Parents always end up with hundreds of seals, which appear on the back of phone-bill payments well into October of the following year.

On Christmas Eve, the

family gathers round to read "The Night Before Christmas" before saying the Rosary. A night dreaming of sugarplums and the Glorious Mysteries passes and children awaken to new bicycles and E-Z Bake Ovens from St. Nicholas. But before the presents may be opened, the pajama-clad children sing "Happy Birthday" to Jesus. The little baby Jesus has been mysteriously born while St. Nick was filling the stockings, and the swaddled figure now lies in the previously empty manger.

Christmas gifts in a Catholic household are meant as a pleasant surprise, not altogether unexpected, yet a treat nonetheless, much like the cherry on a grapefruit half. There might be a new miraculous medal for Mom, or perhaps a Jerusalem Bible for Dad to augment the traditional, secular gifts. After opening the presents, it's time for Mass: no regular Sunday Mass this. The family must leave the house an hour early to ensure adequate seating in the overflowing church. Dad grumbles about people who don't go to church the rest of the year taking seats away from regular Mass-goers. The service lasts twice as long as usual, the organ swells and crashes with a wonderfully resounding intensity, and— for once—everyone is glad to be at Mass.

MIDNIGHT MASS

They begin trickling in around 10:00 P.M., striding determinedly up the center aisle and into the front pews. Look carefully. It's the same crowd that waits patiently at the doors of J.C. Penney a half hour before it opens and that selects prime parking spots at the drive-in before the sun begins to set.

Soon they're joined by the parish choir, robed and ready. The choristers march up to the loft, to prepare themselves for the marathon of pre-Mass caroling that will keep the holy throng attentive until the priest takes over. The organist begins with a droning rendition of "Ave Maria," followed by a medley of old favorites: "Silent Night," "O Little Town of Bethlehem," "Away in a Manger." Occasionally she will vary the tempo and tap out a song in brisk staccato, a technique acquired at the community college's course "Playing Your Home Organ for Fun and Profit." Feeling like extras on the set of *They Shoot Horses*,

Don't They?, the choir sings on and on, until it seems the only holiday tune left unsung is "Jingle Bell Rock."

By this time midnight is growing near and the church is SRO, pews teeming with old faithfuls and families with well-dressed, fidgety children. In the corners of the crowded vestibule are small packs of college kids home for the holidays. They immediately busy themselves comparing exams, cafeteria food and football teams. Midnight Mass is a cool place for a kid to be. One student attends midnight Mass to be seen; an-

other teen is there so that when the rest of his family is at Mass the next morning, he will be free to blast out the new Plasmatics album that sits, clumsily rewrapped, under the Christmas tree.

CATHOLIC FUN DAYS

1. St. Blaise Day (when the priest crosses candles at your throat and prays that you will have a year free of throat disease and choking).
2. St. Patrick's Day

THE FALLIBILITY OF INFALLIBILITY
Changes in Church Rules and Regulations

Many aspects of Catholicism are immutable, designed to last forever. Nevertheless, from time to time the Church changes its customs, laws and institutional structure. Change within the Church, as elsewhere, is inevitably welcome to some people and upsetting to others. The following are some of the major ecclesiastical alterations of our time, along with a sampling of the reactions they have produced.

1. **Change:** Mass said in English rather than Latin.
   Pros: One can actually understand, if not fully comprehend, what the priest is saying.
   Cons: Unlike badly accented Latin droning, inhibits trancelike devotion.
2. **Change:** Altar turned around to face congregation.
   Pros: Congregation can see priest's face and hear better as he celebrates Mass.
   Cons: Same as pros. Also, entails expensive remodeling jobs. Detracts from catatonic contemplation.
3. **Change:** Taking Communion under both species (bread *and* wine).
   Pros: A natural extension of Church doctrine. Reduces artificial distinction between priests and laity.
   Cons: Possibly unsanitary. Alcohol kills germs, but is wiping the chalice lip with the same little cloth after each person's sip really medicinally effective? Some communicants have been

known to make impromptu decisions to receive only the host after realizing who they are standing behind in the Communion line.

4. **Change:** Nuns' habits modified to look less medieval, or abandoned entirely in favor of lay clothing.
   Pros: Nuns seem more human, more effective in dealing with laypeople.
   Cons: You can't tell who's really a nun anymore. Nuns inadvertently get asked out on dates, get sworn at when involved in minor auto accidents.
5. **Change:** Females not required to wear hats or veils to church.
   Pros: Women and girls look more natural, are spared the expense of buying clothing they don't wear anywhere else.
   Cons: Millinery industry decimated, not to mention the Easter parade. Catholic ladies abandon to the women of the British royal family the one fashion territory in which Romans formerly reigned supreme.
6. **Change:** Fasting and abstinence rules greatly relaxed.

Pros: Encourages more natural eating patterns. Eliminates false distinction between "luxurious" meat and "humble" fish.

Cons: Quashes plans for combined crash diet/Catholic conversion program. Those who formerly equated faintness and hunger pangs with signs of piety deprived of a touchstone of their faith.

7. **Change:** Cremation is permitted as an alternative to burial.

Pros: Less expensive, conserves land.

Cons: How will the Good Lord put Uncle Charlie together again for the Second Coming?

8. **Change:** Catholics may now belong to Masonic Lodges without fear of excommunication.

Pros: Reveals enlightened, magnanimous attitude toward formerly anti-Catholic fraternal organizations. Allows Catholics to reap considerable social and economic benefits of belonging to this secret society.

Cons: How will Catholics keep straight so many complicated codes and rituals—Catholic *plus* Masonic?

9. **Change:** Laypeople allowed to preach in church on special occasions.

Pros: Variety enlivens weekly sermons. Expert opinions may be aired. Priests get a well-deserved break.

Cons: Lay preachers don't care how much money parishioners give, so why should they cut short their remarks just because the congregation is squirming with boredom?

10. **Change:** Clergy are allowed to visit taverns.

Pros: One of life's simple pleasures is extended to the clergy. Church acknowledges that despite priestly duties they are people like everyone else. No one should ever drink alone.

Cons: Rectory housekeepers devastated that pastors no longer share after-dinner cordials. Bartenders grumble that barfly priests are horning in on their amateur counselor status, cutting considerably into business.

It is difficult to tell when the Church may initiate changes in other policies—say, the ones concerning birth control. It is instructive, however, to study the first changes in canon law (the official Church code governing Catholic beliefs and practices) since 1917. They required the efforts of almost 200 high Church officials and 1,000 consultants, and involved 6,375 hours of committee meetings. The first draft of the changes was completed in 1981, after 16 years of work, and a final version was not finished until early 1983. The chief results included numbers 7, 8, 9 and 10 above.

What's In	What's Out
Whole-wheat hosts	Hosts made from processed flour
California wines	Jug port aged in church basement for 5 + years
Pink vestments	Black
Felt appliqué banners	Plaster saints
Making your own peace with God	Confession
Wall-to-wall carpeting	Kneelers
Electronic chimes	Real bells at consecration
Flicker-effect lightbulbs	Real votive candles
Hymns sung by congregation	Choirs

Who's Hot	Who's Not
Pope John Paul II	Pope Pius XII
Deacons	Altar boys
Cardinal George of Chicago	Archbishop Weakland of Milwaukee
Mother Teresa	Mother Angelica
Regis Philbin	Conan O'Brien

MYSTERIES OF FAITH

Along with the many well-known theological questions that have plagued the great minds of the Church for centuries (How many angels can dance on the head of a pin?; Can God make a rock He can't pick up?) are more mundane ones that have tormented the minds of Catholic schoolchildren for generations. No nun or priest—not even our parents—has ever been able to answer these questions in a convincing way.

1. Does chewing gum break your pre-Communion fast?
2. What happened to St. Christopher after his de-saintifying?
3. If you go to Mass on Sunday then cross the international date line and go to a place where it's Sunday again, do you have to go to Mass again?
4. What happens if you throw up right after receiving Communion?
5. Do you have to kneel at the consecration when watching the Pope say Mass on TV?

A PROFILE OF POPE JOHN PAUL II

1. Not an Italian.
2. Speaks out freely and often on social issues.
3. Has a strong interest in sports—particularly skiing, hiking, soccer.
4. A published poet (before, not after, election to the papacy).
5. Former actor.
6. Worked in Polish underground during World War II.
7. Allowed an authorized version of his life to be published by Marvel Comics.
8. Traveled abroad more than ninety times so far.

IS THE POPE CATHOLIC!?!

HOW THEY ELECT THE POPE
by Kevin Kelly, Fourth Grade

First the Pope dies. Everyone is sad for a while. Then all the Cardinals fly to Rome and have a party. Then somebody locks every one of the Cardinals in a big room and tells them that they can't come out until they make a new Pope. The Pope has to be one of the Cardinals. The best Cardinal gets to be the new Pope and gets to change his name. Nobody wants to be the new Pope but they don't want to stay in the big room too long either. They argue about who would be a good Pope. Then they all write somebody's name on a piece of paper and throw them into a big furnace. If the smoke comes out black, they all argue about who would be a good Pope again and write everybody's name on a piece of paper and throw it into the big furnace and then it comes out white. A big crowd comes to see the new Pope and wave handkerchiefs at him. They change his name and he comes out and blesses all the people. The Cardinals all fly home till the next time.

CATHOLIC FUN FACTS
Popes in History

DID YOU KNOW THAT . . .*

- There has been only one English Pope?—Adrian IV.
- *You* can be a Pope? It is not a condition of papal election that one be a Cardinal or even a priest to be elected Pope.
- There have been twenty-nine anti-Popes (an anti-Pope is a Pope elected outside the canons of the Church)? One of the most famous is Clement VII who was elected by a faction of French Cardinals who wanted the Holy See to remain in Avignon.
- Of the 264 recognized Popes, 78 are saints? The last to be made a saint was Celestine V.
- The most frequently taken name for a Pope is John (twenty-five times including two anti-Popes but not counting John Paul I or John Paul II)?
- Pope Joan (855–858) is not recognized as a Pope of the Roman Catholic Church?

*Source: *The Reader's Encyclopedia.*

HOW TO BE A LAPSED CATHOLIC

1. *Stop going to church on Sunday.* This is the quickest and most effective way to become a lapsed Catholic. Begin in your teenage years. Refuse to get up for Sunday morning Mass when called by your parents. Roll over, pull the covers over your head and scream that you aren't going and you're never going again. Make sure you have another place to live.

2. *Have an ideological fight with the Church.* Pick out a ruling and find fault with it. Birth control and abortion are topical. Study the issue thoroughly. Talk to your priest and tell him why you can no longer be a practicing Catholic. Repeat what you tell the priest to friends at cocktail parties and clerks at check-out counters. Insist that this is the reason you left the Church and not that you really are not too crazy about going to group Confession.

3. *Join another religion.* Be careful not to *really* join another religion but act like you have. Tell everyone you have decided that Hinduism is older and more in tune with the cosmos. Check Church rulings carefully so you can get back in if the Second Coming gets under way.

4. *Become an agnostic.* This is the intellectual approach. Deduce back to the first cause and become incredibly confused. Cease attending all Church functions with the exception of Bingo until you "get faith."

5. *Dislike the new pastor.* You loved Father Jones/Smith and the new guy talks too loud/ soft and is too Italian/Irish/Polish and never comes to dinner/stops to talk after Mass. Don't worry about going to the neighboring parish; you can dislike that new pastor too.

6. *Have the Church refuse to marry you.* Pick out an atheist and go to pre-Cana. Insist you have no intention of raising your kids Catholic. Tell them you go

at it like rabbits every chance you get and the only reason you want to get married in the Church is to please your future mother-in-law. Storm out in a huff when they tell you you will need some counseling before your wedding banns are published.

The Latin Test

Catholics were bilingual long before it was fashionable or controversial. We could bang out Christmas carols, to say nothing of prayers, in Latin or English. Many of us could rattle off the entire Mass in Latin at the tender age of seven, in plenty of time for our First Holy Communion. But since the abolition of Latin Mass, many Catholics feel as though they have lost a second language.

Here are several Latin phrases to test your memory.

1. *Vivamus Atque Amemus*
2. *Dominus Vobiscum*
3. *Domus Et Placens Uxor*
4. *Donec Eris Felix Multos Numberabis Amicos*
5. *Gratias Agamus Domino Deo Nostro*
6. *Pater Noster*
7. *Paupertas Omnium Artium Repertrix*
8. *Et Cum Spiritu Tuo*
9. *Et Hoc Genus Omne*
10. *Ite, Missa Est*
11. *In Hoc Signo Vinces*

---

1. Let Us Live and Love.
2. The Lord Be with You.
3. A Good and Pleasing Wife
4. As Long as You are Fortunate You Will Have Many Friends.
5. Let Us Give Thanks to the Lord.
6. Our Father
7. Poverty Is the Inventor of All the Arts.
8. And with Your Spirit
9. And All That Sort of Thing
10. The Mass Is Ended.
11. Slogan on Pall Mall Cigarette Packages

V

Catholics at Large

SARACENS, MOORS, DRUIDS AND OTHER NON-CATHOLICS

As children, Catholics are taught that they must be ready to stand up for their faith at any time. It is often not until they reach maturity that they realize this does not so much mean dying bloody martyrdom as explaining to non-Catholic friends that taking the actual body and blood of Christ at Communion really does not have overtones of cannibalism. Little did we expect to be put to this test, because until we left the nest, we never knew any non-Catholics, let alone have to explain things to them. But we did know *about* them.

SO CLOSE AND YET SO FAR:
The Protestants and All Their Sundry Sects

1. *Episcopalian.* Next best thing to being Catholic. High Episcopalians even call priests "priests" and Mass "mass." Catholics might consider attending Episcopalian services under dire circumstances when it is impossible to get to a Roman Catholic Mass on Sunday or a Holy Day of Obligation. For example, you are in the African bush country, in a territory where Church of England missionaries have completely preempted the Jesuits and Maryknollers. The alternative is ancestor worship. Or, you are in a strange city and have slept through all scheduled Catholic Masses. Evensong is an aesthetically appealing, slightly offbeat and upwardly mobile substitute. (Not having checked schedules for Catholic Mass beforehand is a venial sin.)

2. *Congregationalist (United Church of Christ).* Vaguely Christian, extremely liberal. Apparently little or no doctrine. Excellent youth programs (known as Youth Fellowship), leaders of

which may be members of any denomination, agnostics or even secular humanists.

3. **Presbyterian.** Children are admitted to membership when they can pronounce the name.

4. **Lutheran.** It is a well-known fact that Lutherans will try to force Catholic children to renounce their faith. Resisters will be nailed to the door of the nearest Catholic church.

5. **Methodist.** Known for their excellent choirs (see also *Southern Baptists.)* What is the vaunted Method? We never found out by asking our Methodist friends. The only commonly known method in the Catholic Church is the rhythm method.

6. **Southern Baptist.** Their choirs have produced more American pop-music stars than any other sect.

7. **Unitarian.** Like Congregationalist, only more so. They know what they don't believe but have difficulty determining what they do believe. Can't even decide if crosses belong in their churches.*

8. **Christian Science.** The Catholic Church may disallow the birth control pill, but Christian Scientists can't even take an aspirin.*

SECOND COUSINS

9. **Eastern or Greek Orthodox.** Liturgically closely related to Roman Catholicism, but any Church in which priests marry, have children and cultivate long beards obviously has little in common with the One, True Religion. Nevertheless, baklava and Greek coffee after services sure beat Dunkin' Donuts and Maxwell House. It is perhaps in the realm of ecclesiastical fashion that the Greek rite has had the most influence on Catholicism. Orthodox priests were wearing large, clunky, symbolic metal pendants around their necks for centuries before the practice became common among Catholic priests in the 1960s.

10. **Judaism.** As Greece was to Rome, Europe is to America, the hors d'oeuvres are to the entrée, so Jews are to Catholics. Until recently, Catholics were instructed to pray for their conversion.

---

*N.B.: Protestants are not so sure these two are Protestant, but we are.

WAY OUT IN LEFT FIELD

11. *Rastafarianism, Hinduism, Buddhism, Shintoism, Confucianism.* Doctrines so arcane and convoluted not even Catholics can begin to understand them.

THE GREAT GUILT CONTEST:
The Catholics and the Jews

In the contest for the Guilt Championship of the World, the undisputed co-champions are the Catholics and the Jews. Protestant work-ethic guilt, while a contender, just isn't in the same league. Although Catholic guilt and Jewish guilt may appear to be similar, they actually have very different origins. Jewish guilt is generally induced by the Jewish family after the violation of a cultural tradition, such as refusing to take home the extra chicken soup your mother made for you, or becoming a forest ranger instead of a doctor.

Catholic guilt may be related to family disapproval as well, but not in such an immediate sense. The root of all Catholic guilt is the knowledge that every sin committed—past, present or future—adds to Jesus' suffering on the cross. Since virtually anything you do (or don't do) may be a sin, this is a very heavy burden to bear. It's bad enough that you have to pay for sins yourself, but making the Nicest Guy Ever take the rap also is just too awful.

Thus the two outstanding forms of guilt may be summed up as follows. The wayward Jew thinks, "What an awful thing to do to somebody." The Catholic sinner thinks, "What an awful person I am."

MY TURN:
Non-Catholics and What They Think of Us

EPISCOPALIAN, 56, FROM VIRGINIA

After graduating from Princeton, I decided to attend Fordham Law School—a Jesuit institution—because it was one of the few schools offering the specialty I was interested in. I had been forewarned by second-year students that I must take copious notes, because I would be responsible for virtually everything the professors said. I arrived dutifully for my first class, pen and notebook at the ready. I began writing as soon as Monsignor Desjardins, the professor, started to speak. I still have that very first notebook entry of my law school career: "In the name of the Father, and of the Son, and of the Holy Ghost . . ."

JEWISH, 28, FROM MASSACHUSETTS

I never knew much about the Catholic religion but I always enjoyed the customs associated with the holidays, particularly Christmas. I especially liked the life-size nativity scene that was displayed each year on the lawn of St. Mary's, only a few blocks from my house. The figures had been handmade in Italy, I was told, and were very beautiful. Evidently I hadn't appreciated them as closely as I thought I had, as the following incident proves. One night in early December I became aware that the figure of the baby Jesus was missing from the crèche. Incensed at what I thought was an act of wanton vandalism, I immediately called the town police. A Sergeant O'Rourke assured me that the figure of the infant Jesus is never displayed in the crèche until Christmas Day.

PRESBYTERIAN, 45, FROM OHIO

Catholics have way too many children because the Pope won't let them use birth control. He wants Catholics to outnumber everybody else so they can take over the world. Catholics have yellow teeth because they smoke too much. They drink too much, too, and beat their wives and children. The Kennedys make a profit on every bottle of Scotch sold in the United States.

CHRISTIAN SCIENTIST, 29, FROM WASHINGTON

I had just moved to New York and was taking my first bus trip down Fifth Avenue. I was on my way to work on a cold, rainy February morning. The bus stopped in front of St. Patrick's Cathedral and a woman got on with a big black smudge on her forehead. My first thought was that I would discreetly let her know that her face was soiled so that she could take the first opportunity to clean it. But she was quickly followed by a number of other people with similar smudges, and I thought this all must have something to do with a strange New York ritual I knew nothing about. It wasn't until I got to the office, saw someone there with a smudge on her forehead, and asked what it was all about, that I discovered it was Ash Wednesday.

FAMOUS CATHOLICS

The Kennedys	George Carlin	Sean Penn
Joan of Arc	Babe Ruth	Phil Simms
Galileo	Vince Lombardi	Al Pacino
Perry Como	Al Capone	Robert De Niro
Bing Crosby	Sophia Loren	James Cagney
Mary Queen of Scots	Alfred Hitchcock	Martin Scorsese
William F. Buckley Jr.	Ferdinand and	Francis Ford
Al Smith	Isabella	Coppola
Whitey Ford	Napoleon	Martin Sheen
Henry VIII	Fiorello La Guardia	Sammy Sosa
Frank Sinatra	Mussolini	Joe Pesci
George M. Cohan	The San Diego	Pierce Brosnan
Patty Duke	Padres	Liam Neeson
Dean Martin	The Anaheim Angels	Antonin Scalia
Ernest and Julio	The New Orleans	Pat Buchanan
Gallo	Saints	Danny DeVito
Santa Claus	The St. Louis	Spencer Tracy
Bill Murray	Cardinals	Mia Farrow
Michelangelo	Kevin Smith	Ricky Martin
Leonardo da Vinci	Roger Maris	Rosie O'Donnell
Bruce Springsteen	Brooke Shields	Carroll O'Connor

If the quality of a club is indicated by the quality of its members, then we take pride in including lists of famous Catholics, and, even more satisfying, Catholic converts.

FAMOUS CONVERTS

Evelyn Waugh
Betty Hutton
Clare Boothe Luce
Tennessee Williams
Graham Greene
Frances Farmer

But a club is also defined by who's out as well as who's in. . . .

PEOPLE WE WISH WERE CATHOLIC

Albert Einstein
Neil Armstrong
Madalyn Murray O'Hair
The Beatles
All Episcopalians
Abe Lincoln
Muhammad Ali
Albert Schweitzer
Mel Brooks
William Shakespeare
Walt Disney
Walter Cronkite
Gandhi
Michael Jordan
Bill Gates

PEOPLE WE'RE GLAD AREN'T CATHOLIC

Saddam Hussein
Pat Robertson
Ralph Reed
Slobodan Milosevic

EMERGENCY ACTION:
Non-Catholics versus *Catholics*

Let's get down to particulars and examine the very different ways Catholics and non-Catholics respond to critical situations.

A Few Occupations

John F. Kennedy
United States President

Evita Perón
Nation Seducer

Mother Teresa
Nobel Prize Winner and Future Saint

Grace Kelly
Movie Star and Princess

Karol Wojtyla
Pope

1. *Date chokes on chicken bone during dinner*
   NC: Performs Heimlich maneuver
   C: Runs for Holy Oils
2. *Electrical blackout in home*
   NC: Uses flashlight
   C: Lights votive candles
3. *TV breaks down during* Hill Street Blues
   NC: Calls Al's twenty-four hour TV repair
   C: Turns off TV and offers sacrifice to poor souls in Purgatory
4. *Car won't start*
   NC: Calls AAA
   C: Prays to whoever it was who took St. Christopher's place
5. *Breadwinner gets laid off*
   NC: Applies for unemployment

   C: Prepares for seven years of famine
6. *Rowboat springs a leak*
   NC: Bails madly
   C: Attempts to walk on water
7. *Stereo breaks down during party*
   NC: Turns on radio
   C: Passes out hymnals
8. *Food being prepared for multitudes of dinner-party guests burns*
   NC: Calls Chinese take-out
   C: Searches kitchen for a bit of bread and fish to serve
9. *Prize African violet won't bloom*
   NC: Uses Rapid-Gro
   C: Invokes help of St. Jude

SEE NO EVIL

I wish to join the Legion of Decency, which condemns vile and unwholesome moving pictures. I unite with all who protest against them as a grave menace to youth, to home life, to country, and to religion. . . . Considering these evils, I hereby promise to remain away from all motion pictures except those which do not offend decency and Christian morality. I promise further to secure as many members as possible for the Legion of Decency. I make this protest in a spirit of self-respect, and with the conviction that the American public does not demand filthy pictures, but clean entertainment and educational features.

So pledged an estimated ten million Catholics. The Legion's notorious *C* ("condemned") rating was the kiss of death for many films. Catholics were told that attending a *C* movie was a sin. Studios and theater owners were pressured, boycotts were organized and crusades against "condemned" pictures were initiated. Other films were given a *B* ("morally objectionable") rating, and numerous others were cut to fit the standards of the Legion prior to release.

After the early 1960s the *C* rating had little effect on a film's chances for profit, except to boost them. The Legion lowered its profile and changed its name to the National Catholic Office for Motion Pictures. The demise of the organization in 1980 was quiet and not much lamented. The reason given: "Financial considerations."

The U.S. Catholic Conference continues to rate films and to circulate the ratings to the parishes. It is more of an adviser than a censor, however: the *C* and *B* ratings have been abolished and replaced with a simple *O* ("morally offensive").

Below are the Legion's classification system and its rating of several notable films.

THE RATINGS

AI—morally unobjectionable for general patronage

AII—morally unobjection-able for adults and adolescents

AIII—morally unobjection-able for adults

AIV—morally unobjection-able for adults (with reservations)

Class B—morally objection-able in part for all

Class C—condemned

THE MOVIES
Class B

1. *Gone With the Wind* (1939). owing partly to the famous "damn," and also to the ". . . low moral character, principles, and behavior of the main figures as depicted . . ."
2. *Two Faced Woman* (1941). After cuts to avoid *C*.
3. *The Outlaw* (1941). Overexposure of Jane Russell's breasts.
4. *A Streetcar Named Desire* (1951). After cuts.
5. *The Man with the Golden Arm* (1956).

Class C

The Miracle (1951).

The Moon Is Blue (1953). For the use of the words "virgin," "seduce," and "pregnant," and the line "You are shallow, cynical, selfish, and immoral, and I like you."

Baby Doll (1956). Cardinal

Clean Entertainment: The Legion of Decency Hit Parade

Going My Way
Song of Bernadette
A Nun's Story
Miracle at Lourdes
Shoes of the Fisherman
The Trouble with Angels
The Robe
The Sound of Music
Angels in the Outfield
The Bells of St. Mary's
The Singing Nun
Lilies of the Field
The Cardinal
Saint Joan

Spellman denounced from the pulpit of St. Patrick's Cathedral this tale of an undersexed wife and violent, oversexed husband in an unconsummated marriage.

The Pawnbroker (1965)
Blow Up (1966)
Who's Afraid of Virginia Woolf (1966)
Midnight Cowboy (1969)
Fellini's Satyricon (1969)
Zabriskie Point (1970)
M*A*S*H (1970)
Bananas (1971)
Carnal Knowledge (1971)
A Clockwork Orange (1971)
The Last Picture Show (1971)

CATHOLICISM PLAYS A PART

Filmmakers seem to be fascinated by the Church's ritual and drama, its unique lore and lingo. Consequently you've seen many wonderful films that feature the trappings of Catholicism. These ten are simply divine.

Change of Habit. Young nun Mary Tyler Moore gives up the nunnery and regains pageboy hairstyle to have relationship with hip ghetto doctor Elvis Presley, who is surpassed only by Albert Schweitzer and Mother Teresa for selflessness. Tragically, Elvis later succumbs to paganistic rituals, such as playing Las Vegas.

Saturday Night Fever. Faltering though unbearably earnest priest goes to Brooklyn disco with brother, John Travolta, and proves once more that Roman collars are infinitely more attractive than polyester shirts exposing hairy chests festooned with gold medallions.

The Bells of St. Mary's. After two hours of sadistically withholding the truth, Father Bing Crosby tells Sister Ingrid Bergman that the reason she has been ordered to leave the school is not a personality conflict or lack of religious devotion but the fact she has tuberculosis. She is duly grateful.

On the Waterfront. Dedicated, caring priest Karl Malden stands up against the whole mob organization, armed only with faith, an aptly named leading lady, a ripped T-shirt that talks and a pigeon coop.

The Exorcist. Priest Jason Miller gives up life in particularly gruesome fashion for girl who goes on to repeat performances on *The Love*

THE GREATEST STORIES EVER TOLD:

Famous Catholic Writers

St. Augustine
St. Thomas Aquinas
Dante
Gerard Manley Hopkins
G. K. Chesterton
James Joyce
C. S. Lewis
Teilhard de Chardin
Pope John XXIII
Evelyn Waugh
T. S. Eliot
John F. Kennedy
Jack Kerouac

Graham Greene
William Barrett
William F. Buckley, Jr.
Mary McCarthy
John Powers
Andrew Greeley
Pope John Paul II
Joseph Cardinal Bernardin
Mary Gordon
Thomas Merton
Alice McDermott
F. Scott Fitzgerald
Matthew, Mark, Luke and John

Boat. Maybe the devil made her do it. Anyhow, this round to the devil.

The Sound of Music. Tightly knit Catholic family stands up in heroic fashion to the Nazi regime while simultaneously putting on a performance as good as anything the Osmonds, those famous singing Mormons, ever did. Heavy Catholic fantasy content is brought into play when postulant Julie Andrews leaves convent to marry Austrian aristocrat and becomes instant mother of seven without ever (we trust) having had sex.

The Trouble with Angels. Hayley Mills portrays devil-may-care nun-to-be who indefinitely avoids the onset of puberty. Real-life nuns claim this is the result of Hayley's widely publicized two-pack-a-day smoking habit.

The Singing Nun. Debbie Reynolds plays Belgian nun later exiled to Africa because of her commercial success as a recording artist. Unfortunately, Debbie avoids similar fate after accepting this role.

The Song of Bernadette. Features Jennifer Jones as a young girl who beholds a vision in an obscure South American location (ostensibly France) later used in several *Mission Impossible* episodes.

Two Mules for Sister Sara. Shirley MacLaine, as a prostitute in nun's garb, deftly combines the best of two of the world's oldest professions as she contends with banditos and Clint Eastwood's acting.

VI

Infinite Thy
Vast Domain

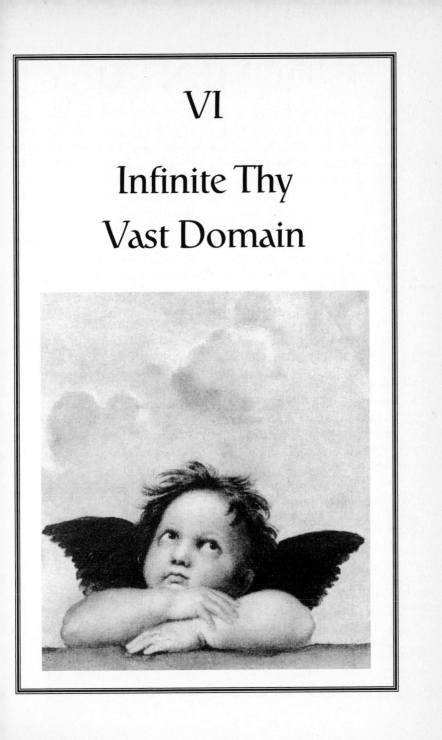

JUDGMENT DAY

Catholics live for the after-life in general and Heaven in particular. Whether or not you will spend your days in Heaven depends on the outcome of your Personal Judgment Day, which in turn depends on what kind of person you have been all your life and, to a lesser extent, if you have friends in high places. When you die, your soul gently floats up to the gates of Heaven where St. Peter, the guardian of the gates, will remind you of every "shut up" you ever uttered to your sister. It's those little things that catch up with you.

Let's say you do pass inspection. There are millions of heavenly souls to meet—fortunately you have all eternity to make their acquaintance. First, seek out the famous inhabitants of the skies. There is God, who gave you the nod at the gates, the Holy Ghost, and the celestial first family: Jesus, Mary and Joseph. You might also make a special effort to locate your patron saint, your guardian angel and old soulmates from Earth. Quickly you'll learn who's who in the heavenly hierarchy and the variations in each level. Seraphim and cherubim, for example: *Vive la difference!* And you'll finally find out what the difference between them is.

You may well be in Heaven because you had a lot of people praying for you while you were sinning away on Earth. Be sure to tell them thanks.

Fortunately you have escaped life as we know it before the hellacious chaos of Final Judgment Day, which comes at the end of the world. What with millions of bodies meeting souls, the mass pandemonium will rival Times Square on New Year's Eve. And the line of impatient folks waiting at the pearly gates will stretch endlessly. St. Peter will surely be rattled. Offer to give him a hand.

HEAVEN

Though folks back from those dubious "near-death experiences" rant endlessly about some tunnel with warmth, love and light radiating from its end, no one ever made it to the warmth, love and light and came back to tell the story. Sure there's faith and what the nuns said was supposed to happen on Judgment Day, but the fact remains . . . no one really knows.

Very probably Heaven is a pleasant medley incorporating life's prime morsels. For instance: 1) an impulsive weekend trip to Las Vegas with an old flame who's run into easy cash; 2) a hugely successful dinner party with only your very best friends in attendance; 3) a jaunt to Disneyland when you have only E tickets and the park is miraculously empty; 4) true, true, true love.

It all sounds heavenly, yet an eternity of such forced celestial celebrations could become trying. Think about it. Day after endless day of "fun" activities—munching meringues, catching up with old friends and reviving that sallowing suntan—forever and ever? Even the thought is a wee bit tiresome. Supposedly your soul will be in such blissful ecstasy just to be with God in Heaven that nothing else will matter. But says who? Will God be insulted if you feel like playing a few sets of tennis or sitting down to a plateful of *pasta primavera*? Surely you deserve it. You wouldn't have made it to the happy hunting grounds if you didn't. Even if you are completely, absolutely, divinely happy just to know God is around, how long will that last? It seems likely that the thrill would slowly dissipate,

Questions We'd Like Answered Before It's Too Late

1. How old are you in Heaven? Do you stay the same age you were when you died, or can you pick an age, say eighteen, and stay that age for eternity?

2. Is there a heavenly hierarchy? Will you really be able to go up to Jack Kennedy and chat? Are people who get to Heaven via Purgatory somehow tainted? Will your Second Grade nun be embarrassed if you had an easier time getting in than she did?

3. What is the protocol if you were widowed and remarried, and now you meet up with both your spouses? Will introductions be awkward and messy? Do you draw straws?

4. What do you wear? Are you stuck wearing the same outfit you were buried in? Will you ever be able to find a facsimile of that fuschia Kenzo jump suit that made you feel like Heaven on Earth every time you wore it?

the way it does for people who finally make partner or win the lottery.

So, no guarantees about what Heaven will be like. Possibly, it *is* everything the nuns said it would be. With thousands of Rosaries under your belt, it had better be.

THE LOSS OF HEAVEN AND THE PAINS OF HELL

Unlike New York City, Hell is not a nice place to visit, nor would you even consider living there. (Many would say that otherwise the two places are just alike, but that is vicious, inaccurate mud-slinging. New York is actually much more like Purgatory.) Hell is a locale whose existence bulks large in the fears and fantasies of the Catholic imagination.

Like other regions of the Catholic cosmology, Hell is a realm of paradox. What Hell is all about is pain, both physical and spiritual. The pain of Hell, at least as envisioned by one fanciful catechism teacher, is equivalent to that of having your arm cut off, then having it miraculously regenerated, then cut off again, and so on, for eternity. But the most terrible pains of Hell are supposedly the spiritual ones a soul suffers because it has been permanently banished from God's presence and grace.

Anyone who has ever given his finger a bad slice with a kitchen knife knows that at that moment the only persons whose absence he cares about are his physician and his mother. One wonders when the poor souls in Hell—writhing in agony—have the opportunity to consider the spiritual pain of their complete and utter fall from God's grace.

Why would you ever bother to spend time in Hell, by all accounts a confusing and extremely unpleasant place? Certainly not because you are told to go there; otherwise there would be no souls left to populate the rest of the cosmological zones. No, you go only if you have to go. That happens if you die in a state of mortal sin, having committed a grievous offense against God and departed this Earth unabsolved, unrepentant and unconfessed. Try to avoid this grisly scenario at any cost. All the teachings and institutions of the Church are there to help and guide you in this endeavor.

Should you be unfortunate enough to end up in Hell, at

Who's Sorry Now?

Herod: tried to kill the Baby Jesus

Nero: threw Christians to the lions

Judas Iscariot: betrayed Jesus

Pontius Pilate: killed Jesus

Martin Luther: started Protestantism

Oliver Cromwell, Henry VIII, Elizabeth I: killed Catholics

Mehmet Ali Agca: tried to kill the Pope

---

least try to make the best of a bad situation. Lucifer, otherwise known as the devil, presides. He was originally one of God's most beloved and powerful angels, but because he chose to do evil he was banished to the netherworld. Never ask him what job he had before his present one. The prevailing climatic feature is extreme heat. Various types of horns are the favored headgear; scaly skins and reptilian tails are frequently seen; and black and red make up the primary color scheme.

You most likely won't have much time to get to know your fellow souls condemned to Hell, between rounds of torture and missing God. With records like theirs, as long as a severed arm, they're probably not your kind of people anyway. At least you always *intended* to do good.

PURGATORY

Purgatory, like traffic court, is a place in which most decent people are surprised to find themselves. They know they don't belong there. They know somebody's made a terrible mistake. They're being treated like criminals for committing a minor offense.

Don't let this happen to you. Unless you take drastic action today, you, like most people, will make a lonnnnng stop in the heavenly green room on the way to your greater reward.

You're a Good Catholic, you say. You go to Mass every Sunday and holy day and receive Communion regularly. You won't die with a mortal sin on your soul, a one-way ticket to Hell. You gather indulgences. You say ejaculations, sometimes thousands of them at a time. You go to Confession. But the sad truth is that no matter how many indulgences you get, you won't get enough. And no matter how many ejaculations you say, you won't say enough. And if you think that five minutes in the confessional and **KAZAMM!** All gone! Well, not so! You're going to pay for your sins before you go to Heaven. And if those venial sins don't seem like a big deal, any of the souls in Purgatory will tell you different. You're playing with fire.

When you get to Purgatory (slightly to the east and somewhat to the south of Heaven) you'll discover it's hot as Hell and probably more crowded. How long will you be there? A long time. How long is long? Who knows? It's the spiritual equivalent of an indeterminate sentence, because the concept of time in Purgatory is somewhat more complex than the theory of relativity. One thing is sure. You will need more than an overnight bag.

But the most important thing to know about Purgatory is that you *will* get out sooner or later. Exactly when is up to you. You can make advance preparation for even-

tual evacuation through the intercession of those you leave behind. Make your family promise to pray for you when you die. Pray for the souls of the faithful departed. Gather indulgences for them. Give alms in their name. Help spring the souls of those dear to you and they will return the favor when they are in Heaven and your time comes.

You can do some things for yourself on Earth—contrition, prayer and good works will go a long way toward cutting down your time in Purgatory. But since there's almost no way to ensure against having to go there at all, let others do the work for you! Have fun on Earth—but be careful, very careful, not to die with a mortal sin on your soul.

INDULGENCES

It is a false question to inquire ... how long purgatory will endure. First, the separated soul no longer lives in the time of this world, but in *aevum*, where duration is not measured in days and years. Second, the soul becomes very conscious of its shortcomings, of the actions it has failed to perform, or performed poorly, or not done at all, and it is wholly intent on making good for these. Thus the intensity of the suffering could well take place in an instant, or could endure for some time, without the soul being aware of it. Because of these considerations theologians have abstained from speculating on the duration of the sufferings of purgatory.

—*The Catholic Encyclopedia*

Bear this in mind when the Church tells you that you will get:

- Three hundred days off for saying "My Jesus, mercy," or "Mother of Mercy, pray for us," or "Jesus, Mary, and Joseph, bless us now and at the hour of our death," or for saying Grace after Meals.
- Five hundred days off for saying "Most Sacred Heart of Jesus, have mercy on us."
- Three years off for saying the Act of Faith, the Act of Hope, the Act of Love or the Act of Contrition.
- Three years off for blessing yourself with the Sign of the Cross; seven years off for using holy water.
- Five years off for saying Hail, Holy Queen.
- Ten years off for saying the Angelus or the Regina Coeli.

LIMBO

There is a misconception held by some non-Catholics that Catholics believe that they and only they will get to Heaven and all others will be consigned to the fiery depths of Hell. This is simply not true. Non-Catholics go to Limbo.

The concept of Limbo is a perfect example of Catholic benevolence toward those who have not found the One True Church. Yes, concept, since no one is quite sure what Limbo looks like and since its very existence has recently been called into question.

Limbo is thought to be a place above Purgatory but below Heaven. In appearance it resembles Heaven and indeed has many of the trappings of Heaven—freedom from care, eternal bliss. So what's so bad about Limbo? Well, it just isn't Heaven. Do the residents know they are not in Heaven? Most likely not, but *we* know they are not in Heaven.

Also eligible to go to Limbo are unbaptized babies, which is why Catholics tend to think of Limbo as a sort of celestial day-care center. Perhaps this vision of Limbo—millions of unbaptized little cherubs dancing in a wooded glen with not a care in the world—was a bit much for the modern Church to take. In any case, the concept of Limbo has been officially abolished. It really is a shame that Limbo is no longer with us, since the new situation puts us right back into the position of being holier than thou. It also presents us with an entirely new set of theological problems, not the least of which is, Where did all those pagan babies go?

YOUR GUARDIAN ANGEL

As a child you are granted a guardian angel. This is your very own "personal" angel who will help you make the right decision in times of near occasion of sin and who will watch over you always. Your guardian angel has a real physical presence and you must make room for him in your pew at Mass and at your desk at school. This can be rather uncomfortable, given the contours of desks at many older Catholic schools.

But you must make small sacrifices for your angel, who combines the vigilance of Mr. French from *Family Affair* with the physical characteristics of Jimmy Stewart's invisible friend, Harvey. For some inexplicable reason, as Catholics grow older the guardian angel becomes less and less prominent in their lives, but whether you know it or not, your own guardian angel is always at your side.

CATHOLIC FUN FACTS
The Trouble with Angels

Did You Know That . . .

- Raphael is known as the sociable angel?
- Each of the 7 archangels is accompanied by 490,000 other angels? Try fitting those on the head of a pin—dancing or not.
- According to various sources there are between seven and ten orders in the celestial hierarchy of angels? Here is a composite listing:

Seraphim
Cherubim
Thrones
Dominions
Virtues
Powers
Principalities
Archangels
Angels

Source: Dictionary Of Angels

Martyrs Matching Column

The society of saints is a closed shop and gaining entrance is not for sissies, as the martyrs can attest. Are you afraid of burning pincers? Wild animals? Raging fires? Then join the Y. Martyrdom is not for you.

Can you match the martyrs with the way they died?

1. St. Sebastian
2. St. Vincent of Saragossa
3. St. Agatha
4. St. Paul Miki
5. St. Saturninus
6. St. Polycarp
7. Sts. Perpetua and Felicity
8. St. Margaret of Clitherow
9. St. Epipodius
10. St. Alexander
11. St. Dymphna
12. St. Lawrence
13. St. Regina
14. Blessed William Horne
15. St. Ignatius of Antioch
16. St. Bibiana
17. St. Ischyrion
18. St. Isaac Jogues

A. *Roasted on a gridiron*
B. *Burned at stake, flames arched over his head, pierced with sword, blood put fire out, still died*
C. *Mutilated and impaled*
D. *Breasts cut off, thrown on red-hot coals*
E. *Scourged, crucified*
F. *Shot with arrows, survived, beaten to death with clubs, body thrown in sewer*
G. *Starved, tied to pillars and beaten with scourges laden with lead plummets*
H. *Pierced with iron hooks, bound on red-hot gridiron, roasted, cast into prison on floor strewn with broken pottery*
I. *Pressed to death under door laden with weights*
J. *Pierced with lances*
K. *Hanged, disemboweled, quartered*
L. *Mauled to death by beasts, beheaded*
M. *Devoured by lions*
N. *Head cut off by her father when she refused to marry him*
O. *Beaten, slashed, fingernails ripped out, tomahawked, impaled, trunk thrown into Mohawk River*
P. *Whipped, scourged, burned with pincers and iron combs, throat cut*
Q. *Stretched on rack, sides rent by iron claws, beheaded*
R. *Starved to death*

Answers:
1. F.; 2. H.; 3. D.; 4. J.; 5. R.; 6. B.; 7. L.; 8. I.; 9. Q.; 10. E.; 11. N.; 12. A.; 13. P.; 14. K.; 15. M.; 16. G.; 17. C.; 18. O.

SAINTS

According to the dictionary, a saint is a person "canonized or officially recognized by the Church as having won by exceptional holiness a high place in heaven and veneration on earth." To Catholics, a saint is someone you try to be like. Well, this is easier in some cases than in others.

IT'S NOT WHAT YOU KNOW BUT WHO YOU KNOW

A careful look through *Lives of the Saints* will show you that many people became saints for doing comparatively little. It seems that the earlier in the history of the Church you lived the easier it was to become a saint. Perhaps the Apostles are among your acquaintances. If so, lucky you, because it seems that nepotism is a sure-fire way of gaining sainthood. To begin with, one can't ignore the fact that *all* of Jesus' friends—every Apostle, Veronica, Barnabas, Joseph of Arimathea, Mary Magdalene and Company—were made saints. But watch out—even after you're canonized you may end up like St. Christopher, desaintified and no longer gracing the dashboards of Catholic automobiles.

In the salad days of sainthood, you were a shoo-in if you:

1. established a religious community (like St. Angela Merici)
2. were the mother of an apostle or major saint (like St. Sylvia, mother of Gregory the Great)
3. were a virgin (like St. Bridget and *many* others)
4. were married to the Blessed Mother (like St. Joseph)
5. were royalty in the right historical period (like St. Ethelbert)
6. were a Pope (like St. Fabian) or
7. were a hermit (like St. Conrad)

No doubt they all did works of charity, prayed continually, had fervent religious dispositions, labored zealously for conversions, led austere lives of self-denial and worked tirelessly for Christ, but these things would probably not earn you sainthood in the twentieth century. One gets the feeling that indulgences weren't the only things being sold way back when, because these good people just don't measure up to those who really earned sainthood.

ABOVE AND BEYOND THE CALL OF DUTY

Beheaded, beaten, roasted, starved, mauled, crucified, hanged and whipped, the martyrs were the ones who really had to sweat for sainthood. With St. Stephen, the first martyr (he was stoned to death), began the noble tradition of going stoically, regally, and even, like St. Lawrence, jokingly to a horrific death in defense of your faith. Were you to be clubbed to death (like St. Peter Chanel) on Staten Island in 1984 for that same glorious reason, no doubt you would be made a saint, but this is not an opportunity likely to be presented to you in our century, devout Catholic though you are.

Saints on the Map Matching Column

1. Genevieve	A. *Poland*
2. Sava	B. *South America*
3. Ansgar	C. *Prussia*
4. Cunegundes	D. *U.S.A.*
5. Casimir	E. *Scandinavia*
6. Nicholas of Flue	F. *Valencia*
7. Judith	G. *Paris*
8. Philip Neri	H. *Russia*
9. Boniface	I. *Lithuania*
10. Bridget	J. *West Indies*
11. Stephen	K. *Sweden*
12. Rose of Lima	L. *Serbian Peoples*
13. Thomas of Villanova	M. *Switzerland*
14. Gertrude	N. *The Americas*
15. Saturninus	O. *Asia Minor*
16. Blessed Virgin Mary	P. *Germany*
17. Our Lady of Guadalupe	Q. *Hungary*
18. St. John	R. *Toulouse*
19. Basil	S. *Rome*

Answers:
1. G.; 2. L.; 3. E.; 4. I.; 5. A.; 6. M.; 7. C.; 8. S.; 9. P.; 10. K.; 11. O.; 12. B.; 13. F.; 14. J.; 15. R.; 16. D.; 17. N.; 18. O.; 19. H.

While it is understandable why people desired blessed martyrdom, some were overzealous in their efforts to achieve it. St. Apollonia, for example, when threatened with being thrown into a fire, jumped in. And St. Pelagia, afraid of losing her virginity to soldiers who had attacked her house, leaped from the roof. While a good martyr is eager to die for her faith, these two ladies were a bit hasty and show a calculated effort to exploit a potentially blessed opportunity. As kindly as the Church may look upon their intentions, these are clearly suicides.

FRIENDS IN HIGH PLACES
Some saints have a special connection to a particular thing, usually an illness or an occupation, and are its patron. For example, St. John Baptist de la Salle set up training colleges for teachers who would instruct the poor; he is the patron of educators. St. Joseph of Cupertino levitated; he is the patron of aviators and airline travelers. In the events leading up to her martyrdom, St. Apollonia had her teeth knocked out; she is, naturally, the patron of dentists.

Some patrons are as lonely as the Maytag repairman. St. Clement I is the patron of marble workers; St. Ambrose, the patron of candlemakers; St. Stephen, stonemasons; and St. John the Baptist, farriers. Their aid is very infrequently implored nowadays, but perhaps after centuries of service they've earned the rest.

Some patrons, on the other hand, are so busy that the responsibility must be shared.

Both St. Yves and St. Thomas More are the patrons of lawyers. Both St. Gennaro and St. Francis di Girolamo are the patrons of Naples. And some patrons have to handle whole cities, countries and even continents single-handedly, like St. George (England), St. Patrick (Ireland) and St. Joan of Arc (France).

VII

Nun Sequitur

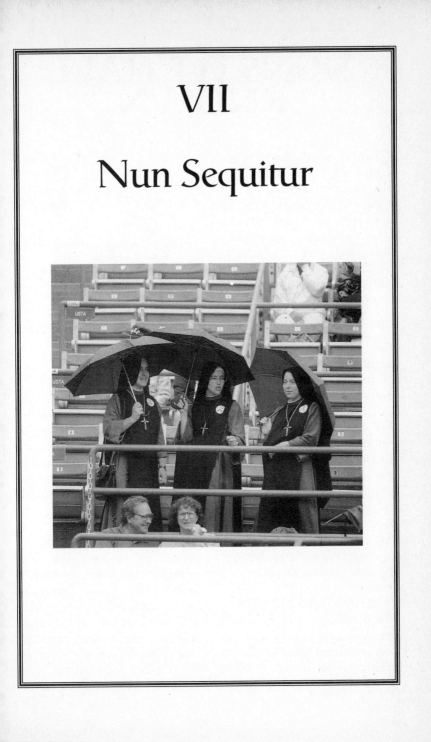

NUNS WE HAVE KNOWN

Simply put, the teaching nuns can be classified in two distinct camps: the nice nuns and the mean nuns. But as anyone surviving parochial school can attest, there are as many nun types as there are Beatitudes. Maybe more. Herewith, a roundup of the most common.

THE PIOUS NUN

This nun believes that anything can be solved by saying a Rosary. Her class prays collectively before class, at lunch, after recess, and at the end of the day. Special prayers are said before tests, during Lent, and on Holy Days. The time Sister lost her grading chart, the whole day was spent offering up prayers to St. Anthony. The pious nun is often an older nun with a sweet, saintly disposition. We all know she's going straight to Heaven.

THE ATHLETIC NUN

She wields a softball bat with prowess and serves a volleyball with a wallop. The athletic nun can be found teaching phys. ed. in many parochial schools. She often takes the name of a fearless male saint, i.e., Sister Stephen Anne, Sister Mary Daniel. She was one of the first to adopt modern garb. This nun is nice, but strict. Even the eighth-grade boys are afraid of her.

THE ANCIENT NUN

Many years ago she was surely an effective, responsive teacher, but those days have come and gone. Sister uses yellowed notes and doesn't notice when her students move the hands of the classroom clock forward to recess time. Every parochial school child has had an ancient nun as a teacher, and every student looks back on that year as the jolliest ever.

THE ULTIMATE NUN

Most parochial schools have a nun that every child adores. She's somewhat strict, but always fair. The ultimate nun likes field trips and will take the class to places like the Coca-Cola bottling plant instead of a boring museum. She goes to all the basketball games and cheers loudly. Everyone wants to sit next to her and cheer, too. Some ultimate nuns can even play the guitar.

THE STRICT NUN

Watch out! According to this nun, every thought, word, or action will land you one step closer to Hell. Solution: Don't think, talk, or do anything unless you absolutely have to, and then be careful. *Never* raise your hand in class, even when you think you know the answer. It's not worth the risk of getting yelled at or rapped on the knuckles. Children taught by a strict nun tend to lapse into panicked silent prayer regularly, and shoot sharp, darting glances around the classroom, keeping an eye on Sister's whereabouts. Parents should watch for early signs of ulcers.

THE YOUNG NUN

A rare breed these days. She is sometimes plain, some- times beautiful, but always perky and enthusiastic. The young nun is a lot like Maria von Trapp. The other teachers like her because she doesn't mind daily cafeteria duty.

TRUE CONFESSIONS
Believe-It-or-Not Nun Stories

SISTER MARY BERNARD

One day a pigeon flew into Sr. Mary Bernard's fifth-grade classroom in a suburb of Detroit. Perhaps it had been attracted by the bread crusts that the children, encouraged by Sr. Mary Bernard, had placed on the windowsills as an act of kindness toward God's wild creatures. The ancient nun had been showing signs of encroaching senility for some time, but the children were taken aback when she clutched her hands to her breast, made a hurried Sign of the Cross, and ordered them to kneel by their desks. As all eyes followed the panicked bird flapping its way wildly around the room, Sister in- formed the class that a miracle had taken place. The Holy Spirit had descended, she said, and they would have to remain in a kneeling position until the Bishop arrived to confirm it. Fortunately, one of the children was sent to fetch the principal, Sr. Clothilde, who told the children to take their seats and assured Sr. Mary Bernard that she personally would take the matter up with the Bishop. The next day the children returned to find a substitute teacher. Sr. Mary Bernard never returned to the classroom.

SISTER CLARE

As every nun knew, school dances were among the nearest of Near Occasions of Sin. Every precaution was taken to ensure that lustful thoughts would not be incited. Girls were required to kneel upon entering the gym to prove that their hems would touch the floor. Gowns were required to have straps (even if spaghetti-skinny), and patent-leather shoes were out. For the ride to and from the dance, girls were encouraged to carry a phone book (to perch upon in case they had to sit on a boy's lap) and a dime to place between their knees. If it fell to the floor, they were to use it to call their parents. Once the music got under way, chaperones circulated around the dance floor, making sure that couples left room for the Holy Spirit between them. For Sister Clare, principal of a high school in Cleveland, however, these precautions were not enough. At the end of every dance, she would require her students to kneel and say an Act of Contrition for the sinful thoughts she was certain they must have had.

SISTER THERESA

In her declining years, Sr. Theresa found it difficult to keep up a full day's teaching schedule in her sixth-grade classroom near Dallas. After lunch, she would direct the boys to read silently from their geography texts, while the girls were instructed to crochet or do needlepoint, the results of which Sr. Theresa would eventually collect and give away as Christmas presents. Two Hispanic girls who knew no English spent the entire day doing handicrafts, producing particularly splendid creations. While her students were thus engaged, Sr. Theresa herself would watch soap operas all afternoon, the black-and-white portable on her desk carefully angled so that only she could see the screen. Occasionally she would spend the afternoon in the cloakroom, carefully starching and ironing the articles her pupils had created, emerging only to rub blue, sticky starch in the face of a misbehaving child. The children did not think to question this routine, or anything else a nun did, in those pre-Vatican II days. Eventually a few parents gathered what was going on, however, and there was reform. From that point on, both boys and girls were given silent reading assignments to last the afternoon, and Sister's only "Guiding Light" came from Heaven above.

SISTER MARGUERITE

During a discussion of career possibilities, one of Sr. Marguerite's eighth-grade boys in Philadelphia had an upset stomach. Knowing he would be refused permission to go to the rest room until the period ended, he tried to ignore the heaving in his middle. Alas, the flu bug got the better of him and he threw up on the floor by his desk. Sr. Marguerite quickly put an end to the minor uproar that ensued. "Now, how many of you said you wanted to be nurses?" she queried, and several girls tentatively raised their hands. "Well, Mary Elizabeth," she said to the most pious of the bunch, "why don't you go get some paper towels and clean up the floor. You're going to be doing a lot of unpleasant things like this as a nurse, and you might as well start learning now."

"I HAD THIS NUN . . ."

Mary Gallo, Queens, New York. I had this nun in the third grade who had been telling us all year about what a horrible person Khrushchev was. He didn't believe in God and he wanted to take over the United States. During the Cuban Missile Crisis her predictions became more and more dire. On the day the crisis peaked, we said our prayers and then Sister Dolorosa told us that Khrushchev was going to blow the world up, probably today. She said we had to be sure to hurry home after school to say goodbye to our parents. In a panic, I ran home at lunch and threw myself hysterically at my mother, begging her to call Daddy at work and tell him to come home before it was too late. My father reassured me that the world was not likely to come to an end that day. When the following morning dawned after all, my mother had her own little blow-up with Sister Dolorosa.

Frances Schmidt, Philadelphia. I was a pretty rebellious kid in high school who got a kick out of breaking the rules, particularly when it came to my uniform. We had a very strict dress code that called for—among other things—blue knee socks and brown loafers. One day I wore black high-tops. Before I had my coat in my locker, Sister Vigilanta swooped over and said to me, "Miss Schmidt, your sneakers tell me you don't care." I told her I didn't know they could talk. I spent the next two weeks in detention.

Patty McGonigle, Cleveland. I went to a very staid all-girls high school with a very boring uniform that I tried to jazz up in any way I could. We had to wear white shirts, gray pleated skirts, and blue blazers. In an imaginative moment, I asked my mother to knit me a blue, white, and gray argyle vest. On the first day I wore it, I was called to the principal's office. Sister Minutiae told me that I was allowed to wear (1) a blue vest; (2) a white vest; (3) a gray vest; (4) a blue and white vest; (5) a gray and white vest; or (6) a gray and blue vest. But I was definitely not allowed to wear a blue, white, *and* gray vest.

Carol Zawicki, Chicago. I attended Marywood Academy, a school with great aspirations to gentility. Before every vacation, we were asked to polish our wooden desks using a product called Pride. One year, just before we went home for Christmas vacation, there came an announcement over the intercom from Sister Immaculata: "Would anyone who has any pride left please report to the principal's office?"

Lorrie Garofolo, San Francisco. Sister Concepción, the geriatric health ed nun at Holy Family High School, was scheduled to tell us about sexually transmitted diseases. She came into the class holding two pamphlets. I could see that one said "Gonorrhea" on the cover; the other said "Syphilis." She held one up and said, "This is this." Then she held the other one up and said, "And this is this." End of lecture.

Anne Lynch, Houston. Sister Debilitata, our French teacher in senior year at St. Dymphna's, was having a difficult time. She was so nervous in front of the class that at times she could hardly speak, let alone *parler*. It was clear to one and all, including Sister, that her grip on reality was tenuous. We took full advantage. One day, one of the girls brought in a clicker, the kind ordinarily used by nuns to call the class to order. She clicked it several times, and as Sister rushed over in alarm, the girl passed it on, so that the next click came from a different part of the room. The class kept a completely straight face. After several repeats of this, Sister was convinced that she was the only one who had heard the noises. That class was the last we saw of her. Eventually, we were told that Sister had gone away. I suppose if this were being made into a movie, it would be called *Driving Sister Crazy*.

Paul Harrigan, Detroit. I never got to school on time in high school. I started every day staring down Sister Punctilius in the late office. She was a scary-looking thing—tall, gaunt, and ancient. "Do I look like a mean old, rotten, vindictive old shrew?" she'd growl. Of course she did. "No, Sister," I'd dutifully reply, afraid she was reading my mind. Then she'd lean over, look me straight in the face, and hiss, "Well, I *am!*" I learned to respect her.

Kate Capelli, Kansas City, Missouri. Sister Horribila, my favorite fourth-grade nun, warned us not to do two things: tease our hair or drink out of public water fountains. If you wore big teased hair (which we weren't going to do in fourth grade anyway), bugs would drop in it, build their nests, and have babies in your hair. She knew someone it happened to. And if you drank from public water fountains you could swallow a snake egg, which would hatch in your stomach and grow. The snake would have to climb up your throat to get out. She knew someone it happened to. The doctors had to put trays of food in front of the woman so the snake would smell it and come out. But when the snake began to come out, a nurse got so scared she screamed. The snake bit the lady and she died. Sister knew someone it happened to, of course, although no one else ever did.

EYES IN THE BACK OF HER HEAD:
The Nun's Point of View

The legend persists that nuns have a sort of sixth sense in the classroom, an uncanny ability to detect even the smallest infraction of the rules, almost as if they had eyes in the back of their heads. Here is one nun's account of how she went about establishing this legend among her students:

I was substituting for a few days for a Sister who'd taken a much-needed spiritual retreat. I'd heard that this particular class was a rough group, and I knew I'd have to take control right away, otherwise the classroom would have been a living . . . well, I would have had to go on a spiritual retreat myself. As I approached the classroom, I could hear a sort of dull, ugly roar even in the hallway, as if several Christian martyrs had just been thrown to the lions. If ever I were to join their hallowed ranks, I vowed, it would not be that day.

As I proceeded to my desk at the front of the room, I maintained a steely silence. With a stiff wimple under my chin, I couldn't help but hold my head high and proud. And the long black veil hanging down over the sides of my face kept the little hooligans from seeing that I was glancing discreetly around the classroom, searching for anything that would help me not merely to survive, but to prevail, in this most hostile of environments.

Out of the corner of my eye, I noticed a wadded-up piece of paper—by the sticky look of it, a humongous spitball—lying on the floor near a desk in the back row. Before proceeding to the blackboard to write out my

name and the day's assignments, I glanced at the alphabetical seating plan. The student nearest to the spitball was Malone, Thomas. Naturally, Tommy Malone was not the student in that seat at the moment. After all, I didn't take my vows yesterday. Mixing up the new Sister by playing musical chairs was the oldest trick in the book.

As I began to write "JMJ" at the top of the board, I said casually, "I hope everyone is in the correct seat. Because I have some special after-school work in the church neatening up candle wicks for anyone who isn't in the right seat by the time I finish writing out this assignment." After the shuffling and scraping died down, I kept on writing for several more minutes, never once looking back at the class. Just as I was finishing up, I said in the same offhand tone of voice as before, "Would Thomas Malone please pick up the piece of paper lying next to his desk and deposit it in the wastebasket?"

As I turned around, a loutish lad with an awestruck look on his face lumbered down the aisle and reverently placed the wad in the can. From there on in, I had very few problems.

THESE FOOLISH THINGS REMIND ME OF YOU:
What We Miss About Nuns

Today's nun is, as often as not, an uptown woman, consulting her PalmPilot for her next appointment, stopping by the manicurist to fix a broken nail on her way to a lunch date, then dashing back to work. She dresses stylishly, though her wardrobe may contain a few more navy-blue outfits than the national average. A cross around the neck used to be a surefire way to tell a nun from a non, but that test is no longer reliable. You have to look closely to see the pin on her lapel.

But it's not appearance alone that sets present-day nuns apart from their sisters of yore. The real difference is that today's nuns aren't scary, which makes them a whole new breed. With a residual anxiety that has been tempered by the passing years, many Catholics look at nuns differently today. They feel privileged to have been taught by some of these extraordinary women, and fondly remember the little things about nuns—things their children will never know.

Their eyeglasses	Their "wedding" rings
Their soapy scent	Their soft hands
Their smooth skin	Their deep pockets
Their starched habits	Their calm voices
Their scrubbed faces	Their fountain pens
Their flowing skirts	Their names
Their shoes	Their handwriting
Their pitch pipes	The creases in their veils
Their wraps	

HOLY APPELLATIONS!
The Most Colorful Orders of Nuns and Priests

Nuns

Benedictine Nuns of the Primitive Observance
Carmelite Sisters of St. Thérèse of the Infant Jesus
Daughters of Divine Charity
Little Missionary Sisters of Charity
Sisters of Charity of Our Lady, Mother of Mercy
Cistercian Nuns of the Strict Observance
Servants of Our Lady Queen of the Clergy
Daughters of the Cross
Sisters of the Holy Cross and of the Seven Dolors
Augustinian Daughters of the Crucified
Daughters of St. Francis of Assisi
The Poor Clares
Sister Servants of the Holy Spirit of Perpetual Adoration
Handmaids of the Precious Blood
Servants of the Holy Heart of Mary
Sister Servants of the Holy Ghost and Mary Immaculate
Congregation of the Incarnate Word and the Blessed
     Sacrament
Nursing Sisters of the Sick Poor
Little Sisters of Jesus
Poor Handmaids of Jesus Christ
Sister Adorers of the Precious Blood
Sisters of Our Lady of Charity of the Refuge
Company of the Savior

Priests

Augustinians	Marist Fathers	Redemptorists
Benedictines	Maryknoll	Salesians
Carmelites	Fathers	Somascans
Cistercians	Oratorian	Sulpicians
Dominicans	Fathers	Trappists
Franciscans	Pallottines	Trinitarians
Holy Ghost	Premonstraten-	Vincentians
Fathers	sians	Xaverians
Marian Fathers	Resurrectionists	

Nuns Say the Darndest Things:

"No."
"Woe betide you!"
"Bold and brazen."
"Kiss it up to God."
"Offer it up."
"You're putting another nail in the Cross."
"Line up in size order."
"You're my cross to bear."
"I'll just wait until you're ready. We have all day."
"Did you bring enough gum for everyone in the class?"
"Keep your eyes off your neighbor's paper."
"No."

PRIESTS WE HAVE KNOWN

FATHER HOLE-IN-ONE
"Being a Catholic is like learning to play the game of golf. It's something you can do for a lifetime and never get right. Oh, but the hope of a hole-in-one or a perfectly executed sandblast keeps us going." So begins a typical sermon by Father Hole-in-One. Long the pastor of St. Burning Tree by the Water, he looks forward to Sundays as his day to wrest the clubs from his bag after celebrating 12:30 Mass. In an imperfect world, Father finds a few perfect hours on the links with his new set of Ben Hogans and his Top-Flites. He feels communing with nature and his six-iron brings him closer to HIM. Father's language on the course, however, can be spicy. "Mother Mary," he shouts as an errant drive strikes a tree.

"Oh, take a Mulligan," his trusty golfing partner, the Bishop, chortles. "Saints be praised," Father Hole-in-One gasps, after negotiating a tricky downhill putt for his double-bogie. "Christ!" he screams as the foursome behind them drives a ball right over their heads. "Father, forgive them," the Bishop snickers, rising to his feet. "They know not what they do!"

FATHER HAVE-A-NIP

Jolly, red-faced Father Have-a-Nip is a saintly man who forever seems to have a small smile glued to his countenance. Never known to be fond of the early Masses, he does, however, have an excellent relationship with the congregation. Rather than try to hash out all the parish problems on the front steps of the church, Father has an open-door policy at the rectory, where his equally saintly housekeeper, Mrs. Rottenelli, keeps his study amply stocked with refreshments. Father is not against any member of the parish coming over after Mass to have a few belts and to unburden his heart. Father also knows that good Irish or Scotch whiskey is a great tongue loosener for the troubled in his care. He is partial to any of the Johnnie Walkers, but is only really in Heaven when one of the faithful sends him a bottle of Glenlivet at Christmas. While having a nightcap or two, Father has been known to captivate family gatherings for hours with his stories of traveling across the country by train with the Archbishop.

FATHER FIRE-AND-BRIMSTONE

Many members of Father's small parish in Kansas think the Good Father was dropped on his head as a child. For what else could account for his graphic descriptions of the tortures of Hell? The way Father talks at Mass, you would think he had already been there.

Some of the more wry among his parishioners have taken to numbering his sermons. "The Omen III, the Last Gospel" was one of their favorites. It began with Father giving a suitable Lenten address and then quickly admonishing the group to imagine the worst possible thing they could. Children contemplated no candy for a month, and adulterers imagined discovery. Father just stood at the pulpit tapping his toe and smirking. After five minutes of silence, he asked quietly, "Are you all imagining the worst thing that could happen to you?" The congregation nodded. "Well," Father fairly screeched into the microphone, "that's what Hell is like! Years and years and eons and eons of the worst possible thing you could imagine. Centuries and millenniums! Con-

stant, everlasting, continuing, without end! The worst thing you could imagine! I hope I have made my point."

FATHER STRUM-A-TUNE
In the sleepy parish of the Church of Holy Civil Disobedience, not far from the campus of the University of California at Berkeley, resides a throwback to those halcyon days of protest marches and felt-appliqué vestments. He is Father Strum-a-Tune, and he remembers the 1960s as a time when right was right, wrong was wrong, and priests were as likely to be marching with Dr. King as scribbling soon-forgotten sermons in the rectory. In fact, Father Strum-a-Tune joined the priesthood in order to bring a new social conscience to the flock.

Among Father's many accomplishments—which often landed him in the pages of national news magazines—were the "Jazz Mass" for folk guitar, the national best-seller *God Doesn't Have a Draft Card*, and his famous "Eat, Drink, and Be Mary" sermon, which celebrated both natural grains and celibacy.

But Father Strum-a-Tune may be a dinosaur in today's world, sitting in his book-lined study fingering well-worn pages of Thoreau and Teilhard de Chardin. Humming "Michael Row the Boat Ashore" and drawing up plans for a geodesic dome church, Father awaits the day when social consciousness will again be raised and his flock will once more march to the beat of a different drummer.

IN GOD'S HOUSE

Catholic schoolchildren spend half their lives in church. The hour on Sunday that generates weeping and wailing from adults is only a drop in a very big bucket for parochials. In the life of a Catholic schoolchild, Mass can take place at any time and for almost any reason. Witness the Graduation Mass, the Opening-of-School Mass, or, worst of all, the Somebody-Important-Died Mass. If that Important Somebody happened to be a priest or a nun, or, God forbid, a Monsignor, you were in for an affair that made *Gone With the Wind* look like a short subject.

But the Masses that were being said for *you* were far and away the most rigorous, and for many good reasons. First of all, you knew you didn't really have to be there. The Guy in Charge had not asked/demanded your presence; no mortal sin would appear on the clean milk bottle that was your soul if you didn't appear. But since this type of Mass usually took place during school hours, getting out of Alcatraz would have been easier than getting out of going.

Secondly, you knew that Sister was making an enormous sacrifice for you. After all, she'd given up *everything* in life just to teach you, and she was taking time away from the most important thing in the world to pray for your unworthy, and usually ungrateful, soul. You knew that anything that got you excused from school was Mighty Important. This knowledge demanded extra holiness.

Lastly, this was one of the few occasions when your demeanor at Mass was being closely scrutinized by the Blackskirts. If their inspection revealed one turn of the head, one yawn, or the tiniest little whisper to your neighbor (who was, after all, seated a foot away, next to the space you left for your Guardian Angel), you were ruined.

The runner-up to Mass for time-in-church consumption was rehearsal. Catholic schoolchildren rehearsed for everything—processions, First Holy Communion, Graduation, Confirmation, and sundry other rituals—several times. The process of lining the class up in size order alone could take hours. And once that was accomplished, we rehearsed walking down the aisle at just the right pace and with just the right amount of space between ourselves and the person in front of us, stopping at the pew assigned to us, genuflecting, entering the pew, moving to the spot in the pew assigned to us, kneeling down, and staying motionless until Sister's clicker told us we were all in place and could sit.

Since one absolutely did not turn one's head from the altar, if Sister had not signaled to us by clicking or clapping, we would be kneeling still. These rehearsals were enlivened when singing was part of the program.

Although this came around only seasonally, the all-around fave reason for being herded into church was to say the Stations of the Cross each Friday in Lent. *Nothing* in life could match the Stations for high drama, pathos, and overall catharsis. Particularly sympathetic sobs were heard when the altar boy intoned, "Veronica wipes the face of Jesus." She was a Regular Person. It could have been *us*. And haughty indignation was rampant as Jesus fell three times. If we had been there, we would have helped Him.

Altar boys were in a class by themselves in the time-in-church sweepstakes. In addition to their duties at Sunday Masses and on Holy Days of Obligation, altar boys served at Nuptial Masses, put in time before school began (serving predawn Masses attended only by the frighteningly pious), and were frequently released from class to serve weekday Funeral Masses.

A DAY IN THE LIFE OF A PAROCHIAL SCHOOL CHILD

8:15 A.M.   Bell

8:15.5 A.M.   Children silently line up in front of their class-
                 rooms—boys in one line, girls in another,
                 shortest to tallest, one arm's length apart.

8:16 A.M.   Hands over hearts, the children say the Pledge
                 of Allegiance as the flag is raised. They are
                 grateful to live in the land of the free and the
                 home of the brave.

8:19 A.M.   No, there are no crickets on the playground. It's
                 Sister with her clicker. Each line marches into
                 a classroom.

8:20 A.M.   Informal inspection by Sister. Uniforms spot-
                 less? Socks pulled up? Fingernails clean? Gig-
                 gle potential high.

8:25 A.M.   Morning prayers. Just one decade of the
                 Rosary this morning. Shannon Ryan forgets
                 her Rosary and has to borrow one from
                 Sister.

8:35 A.M.   Religion. Pop quiz on questions from the *Balti-
                 more Catechism*. No one can explain the Eighth
                 Commandment. Sister looks peevish.

9:15 A.M.   Arithmetic. "If three loaves and five fishes were
                 multiplied five hundredfold, how many of each
                 would there be?"

10:00 A.M.   Sister's clicker clicks. Recess. The sole purpose of recess is to allow children to use the bathroom. They are permitted to talk at will, and revel in their freedom.

10:15 A.M.   Back to the classroom for a quick Our Father, Hail Mary, and Glory Be.

10:20 A.M.   Science. Sister explains the root systems of vegetables as her students insert celery stalks in beakers of colored water. All vegetables are gifts from God.

11:00 A.M.   Surprise visit from Father! Everyone sits up straight and Sister beams and wipes the chalk dust off her hands. Father discusses vocations, and by the time he leaves everyone thinks that maybe they do have the calling.

11:55 A.M.   Sister's clicker clicks and all rise to say Grace Before Meals.

12:00 noon   Lunchtime. It's hot dog day! The cafeteria ladies also serve beans, cole slaw and half-pints of whole milk. David Cooney eats four hot dogs and has to go to the nurse's office.

12:30 P.M.   Recess. Boys practice hoops. Girls jump rope. Sister reprimands "roughhousers."

1:00 P.M.   Recess ends. Lines file back into classrooms. Sister leads Grace After Meals.

1:03 P.M.   Social Studies. The class reads about Kara and Jimi, island children who live in the South Seas. Kara and Jimi are not Catholic. That is why we must support the mission.

1:30 P.M.   Spelling. Today's spelling bee includes the words "transubstantiation," "Confiteor" and "monstrance."

2:00 P.M.   P.E. Gym shorts have been worn under uniforms, so boys remove their pants, girls their jumpers. Teams are picked and a vicious game of kickball ensues. Liz Evans falls and chips her front tooth.

3:00 P.M.   Uniforms back on. One more decade of the Rosary to end the day.

3:15 P.M.   Final bell rings. Orderly exit from classroom under Sister's watchful eye, but flight through schoolyard resembles scene from *Wild in the Streets*. Joyous din can be heard for blocks.

VIII

Am I Still
a Catholic?

THE FIRST HOLY COMMUNION CLASS OF 1965:
Where Are They Now?

F. X. O'Donnell
Accountant at Big Eight firm. Total workaholic. Engaged to a cute paralegal. Doesn't wear socks with his loafers on weekends. Makes a mean margarita. Hasn't been to Mass in years.

Patrice Anne Malinowski
Benign dermatologist by day, writer of horrific medical thrillers by night. Excelled in biology at St. Anne's Girls' High. Single, but looking. Hit-or-miss Mass-goer.

Mary Elizabeth Barrett
Modern dancer in experimental dance company in San Francisco. Shares a loft with three friends. Attends Mass only when visiting the folks in Boston. Believes that the discipline instilled in her by the nuns accounts for her ability to endure the extreme sacrifice and pain associated with a career in dance.

John Vincent Minnelli
Semipro football player. Got his start on the playing fields of Our Lady Queen of Heaven Parish. Wears a gold cross on a chain around his neck. Attends Mass regularly. Married, has one child who attends parochial school.

THE WAY WE WERE

THE CATHOLIC MAN

The quintessential Catholic man is married. He's tall and handsome, and wears a suit and a hat. The hat is really important. He works for an insurance company, and has a nice wife named Margaret who always wears an apron and has a martini and meat loaf ready for him when he comes home. He walks in the door every night at 5:30, and looks forward to it. Gallivanting around after work not only doesn't appeal to him, it would never *occur* to him. He has four well-scrubbed, very obedient children, the youngest of whom he diapers and puts to bed at night. His station wagon is full of toys, tissues, and coloring books. He has no desire to own a new, black BMW—he couldn't fit the kids or the groceries in it. He likes to barbecue for his family on the weekends, and wears a red-checkered apron that makes his children laugh. He likes going to Mass with his kids on Sundays, and wears a suit and tie because he's an usher. Afterward, so Mom can get some peace and quiet, he takes them to the park or even to meet an ancient nun who taught him math in high school.

The quintessential Catholic man is holy, but in an understated way. He takes his religion seriously, but doesn't make a show of it. The only outward sign of his faith is the Miraculous Medal he wears, or the Rosary on his dresser. You know he believes, though, because he'd never miss Mass and goes to confession regularly.

THE CATHOLIC WOMAN

The quintessential Catholic woman's life revolves around the Church. She has numerous children, and spends a good part of her day taking them to school and picking them up again, helping them with their homework, cooking their dinner, doing their laundry, and generally cleaning up after them. But the rest of her time is devoted to the parish.

She volunteers in the playground at lunch and in the school library in the afternoon. After dinner, she goes to meetings of the Mothers' Club or the Rosary-Altar Society. She sells tickets to the parish dances, visits a sick or elderly parishioner, takes Sister to the market, and cleans the altar. Yet she somehow finds time to say the Rosary with her family at least once a week and to slip in an early morning Mass occasionally, all the while keeping track of days of fast and abstinence and Holy Days of Obligation. She is the bedrock on which the parish church is built.

The quintessential Catholic woman has little time or energy for pampering herself. She usually does her own hair and economizes on her wardrobe. She never gets a manicure, though polish adorns her nails sporadically. With her big family, money is often tight, and she has to make a little go a very long way. She is the last person she

thinks of or does anything for. The effects of the Me Generation have not filtered down to her, and probably never will.

THE CATHOLIC BOY

Sister Mary Perpetua yells out that he's bold and brazen. His mother calls him "all boy." Father Fitzgibbon says he's a smart aleck. We're talking about the quintessential Catholic boy.

In school the quintessential Catholic boy walks a fine line. He knows how to act bad enough to have fun, but not so bad as to get into trouble. He's taught himself to mimic filmstrip beeps, which results in Sister advancing the filmstrip too quickly. When the class is sitting in the dark watching a film like *Photosynthesis and You*, about ten minutes of audio is left when the visual part has finished.

Sister is confused. The class is delighted.

On the playground the quintessential Catholic boy hangs out and shoots baskets with the other guys. He's a forward on the Blessed Sacrament team, and would have been a starter this year but the coach is still mad at him for starting a bonfire in the trash can behind the gym last year.

A couple of days a week the quintessential Catholic boy rides his bike to the nearby grocery store, where he is employed as a "bagger" after school. He puts on his green apron and "Hi, How May I Help You?" button and packs groceries, making sure not to squash the bread with the canned corn.

And, of course, the quintessential Catholic boy is an altar boy. He's conscientious and takes his job seriously, but is not above tucking some incense into his pocket before leaving the sacristy.

Our quintessential Catholic boy is no angel. But despite his mischievousness, he has a pretty good chance of eventually getting to Heaven.

THE CATHOLIC GIRL

Virtually every Catholic girl goes through a stage of complete and utter goodness sometime between the ages of eight and twelve. This phase, which lasts anywhere from a few days to several months, is known as the "I want to be a nun" stage. It is at this point that a merely ordinary child is transformed into the quintessential Catholic girl.

She is a model student. When a classmate asks to copy her homework she says no, but offers to stay with him after school to explain the math equations. When Sister leaves the classroom for a few minutes, the quintessential Catholic girl—because she is the one who seems closest to nunhood—will be asked to watch the class and report any transgressions.

At home the quintessential Catholic girl helps Mom with the dishes, quiets sibling squabbles, and sets the table without being asked. The only time she loses her temper is when her little brother goofs off and refuses to take Mass seriously. In extreme cases, she is known to fast for days at a time, offering up her hunger for the poor souls in Purgatory. Every night before going to sleep she prays fiercely, often for the victims of a natural disaster or for other people she doesn't know.

The slide back to non-quintessential Catholic girlhood behavior often coincides with a blossoming interest in either horses or boys.

WHAT GOES AROUND, COMES AROUND

You pass a school playground filled with laughing children, all neatly dressed in their white shirts and plaid jumpers or navy pants. A typical Catholic school? Guess again. It's one of a small but growing number of public schools that have copied parochial schools and adopted mandatory uniforms for their students.

Maybe those uniforms weren't the most unfashionable things on the planet, but that's what parochial school girls always thought of them. Whether green plaid or blue serge, pleated skirt or bibbed jumper, uniforms were a daily penance to be endured, as was the taunting by the public school girls who seemed to have dozens of stylish school dresses.

But now, all these years later, the score is evened out. The public school uniforms are every bit as ugly as the Catholic ones were. The public school authorities seem to have passed up the beanie, however, a decision understood and applauded by even the most hard-hearted parochial school girl, who wouldn't wish one of those creepy little caps on her worst enemy.

REASONS TO REJOIN THE CHURCH

Maybe you were away for a long time, and maybe there were some pretty serious disagreements. Now you want to patch things up again. Just remember that the Church has changed, too, and that things won't be exactly the same as when you left. Try not to be too upset about this. Isn't that why you left in the first place—because things never changed? Here are a host of honorable and merely convenient reasons to come back into the fold.

1. It's respectable to have a religion again.

Do-your-own-thingism is definitely over, even in the spiritual realm. You want something solid, something with tradition, something hard-boiled. Something that looks substantial on college applications, army dog tags, and hospital admittance forms. You want a religion that says, "We treat sinners the old-fashioned way—we burn 'em!" For those on the rise in business and politics, nothing bespeaks wholesomeness and dependability of character like church membership. Caution: If you are looking for respectability only, become an Episcopalian.

2. If you must continue to dissent, there's a lot more tolerance than there used to be.

In fact, it's very hard these days to get thrown out for being a free-thinker, since the clergy and religious tend to be much more liberal than the laity. Let's just not go over the top like the Dutch and start throwing things at the Pope.

3. It's a great excuse for leaving boring Saturday night parties early.

Even if you later decide to throw a movie on the VCR or go out dancing at an all-night club, you can still catch the 5:30 Mass on Sunday afternoon.

4. As a regular Mass-goer, you'll be more welcome at the big holiday services everyone and his brother wants to attend.

5. If you're a diehard fan of the Latin Mass, you can probably search out a parish offering an approved version of the ancient rite.

Just don't be surprised when your references to any post-1965 phenomena—such as Watergate, the space shuttle, or "Wheel of Fortune"—are met with a blank stare from fellow parishioners.

6. The priests give better sermons.

They've got to draw crowds these days, like the poor Protestant ministers always had to do to keep their jobs.

7. To get married.

If it's just to please your parents, it doesn't count.

8. To get your baby baptized.

This always counts. Even if you choose not to save your own soul from going to Hell, you've saved baby's soul from going wherever it would go now that it no longer goes to limbo.

9. You're very unlikely to happen upon a Guitar Mass these days.

Tradition is back in music, too. If you're really lucky you'll get a well-drilled choir singing motets or Gregorian chant. At worst, you'll have to endure "Pachelbel's Canon" on the organ.

10. The Sacrament of Reconciliation.

It used to be called Confession. You don't have to recite every little peccadillo to the priest anymore in order to have your sins absolved. It's done en masse, for you and the rest of the congregation. If this is a little too generic for your taste, individual consultation is still available upon request.

11. The Second Coming might be coming sooner than you think.

Still the biggest and best reason of all. "*I*   t was in the beginning, is now and ever shall be . . ." Amen.

The Guardian Angel
"A Top Catholic Magazine"

CONTENTS

A Word from Me
FR. BILL

ARTICLES

BACK TO THE FUTURE
If we could travel back in time to the days of Christ . . .

THE INQUISITION
Time for a New One?

IF MY PRIEST GETS MARRIED . . .
Is He Still My Priest?

AMERICAN CATHOLICS
Whose Church Is It Anyway?

THE METHODISTS
Who are they?

NUNS IN OUR SCHOOLS
Where are they?

FEATURES

THE NEW DRIPLESS CHALICE
Hygiene Comes to Communion

INSIDE THE KINDER, GENTLER VATICAN BANK
Is the Collection Money Safe?

TV PRIESTS
A Vanishing Breed

MY FRIEND THE RABBI
I can't hold it against him . . .

"I KILLED MSGR. KILKENNY"

THE NOVELS OF FR. GREELEY
Did a priest write this?

PROFESSIONAL SPORTS AND PRAYER
Is making the Sign of the Cross during a game "just showing off"?

FICTION
Bless Me, Father

DEPARTMENTS
THE BOOKWORM
THE INTERVIEW
THE MATINEE

A WORD FROM ME
by Fr. Bill

Many of you have written to tell me that your faith is frequently tested by the slings and arrows of outrageous fortune, or just to say you are not having an easy time of it. When you are finding it difficult a sense of humor comes in mighty handy. Our Lord had a sense of humor and there are many examples in the Scriptures of the Apostles yukking it up when the going got rough.

It is during these trying times when you must lift your chin up, throw your shoulders back, and pull your stomach in. Then let out a really good laugh. A real belly laugh. After you do this a few times you will find that laughter actually comes very easily. Soon you will find that you can laugh at almost anything. Keep laughing until your knees buckle and you are red-faced and convulsed on the floor. After you pick yourself up, you will find that things don't seem quite so desperate as they did just a few minutes ago, and you can then approach your faith with a renewed vitality and sense of perspective.

MY FRIEND THE RABBI
"I can't hold it against him . . ."

I have known Sidney Green as long as I can remember. Back in Brooklyn, Sidney and I would play stickball in the street, sneak smokes behind the malt shop, and try to avoid the bullyboys who forever seemed to be tormenting us. But early in our friendship I realized that Sidney and I came from different worlds.

He didn't go to our school, for one thing, and everyone I knew went to St. Anne's. Sidney also wore funny hats, even on real cold days, and I used to yell at him from down the street, "Hey Sidney, your hat ain't got no flaps!"

But the thing that really clued me in to how different we were was that Sidney used to put on his funny hat with no flaps and go to church on Saturday. Going to church on Saturday *(cont'd on page 12)*

"I KILLED MONSIGNOR KILKENNY"
by Tommy Rinaldi

It was a Tuesday in Lent. I was an altar boy and a basketball player. I decided to go over to the church during the lunch hour to say the Stations of the Cross. The whole school did the Stations every Friday. But that day, I was feeling kind of holy and went on my own.

This was not strictly allowed by the nuns. Several students had seen statues in the Church weeping and moving, so we were confined to the schoolyard during recess. But I thought I couldn't get into that much trouble for praying. As it turned out, there would soon be tears in that church, but it wouldn't be the statues that were crying.

I had gotten to the Third Station. Like other kids, I was totally empathizing with Jesus' suffering. In fact, on Fridays, by "Veronica Wipes the Face of Jesus," all the girls were crying. I wasn't yet, but I was deeply moved. So moved that I didn't notice what must have been the shuffle of Monsignor Kilkenny's ninety-year-old feet as he made his way out of the confessional where he had been napping, as he was wont to do. Evidently, he didn't notice me either, because as I genu-flected in front of "Jesus Falls the First Time," he tragically tumbled over my kneeling frame.

Heaven help me. Monsignor never recovered from the injuries he sustained, although he lingered for three days before succumbing. Most Precious Blood put on the biggest extravaganza in its history for his funeral. They took us out of school to go to it, every single kid. Monsignor was laid out at the front of the church in an open coffin. And if that wasn't the scariest thing any of us had ever seen, he was propped up so that wherever you were sitting you were looking right at the face of a dead guy. Some of the first graders have never gotten over the shock.

And neither have I. To this day, I am known in Most Precious Blood parish as The Boy Who Killed Monsignor Kilkenny.

HOLLYWOOD'S HEAVENLY HITS:
Movies About Catholics

MOONSTRUCK. Cher plays an Italian-American widow who cheats on her fiancé with his brother and then goes to Confession to clear her conscience. Nowadays, it is more likely the priest would confess to Cher that he was having an affair with her fiancé's sister.

THE MISSION. Men of the cloth force their customs, rituals, and drab earth tones on a group of unsuspecting innocents. No, this is not a documentary on parochial school education, but the story of a Catholic missionary in the South American jungle.

SISTER ACT. Another entry in the "hardened ex-con hides out in convent and undergoes miraculous transformation" genre. The only miraculous thing here is that this may be the first movie in history to waste Maggie Smith's talent. Uses Motown score and features nuns singing "My Guy" as "My God." Thank God they didn't hit Broadway—we might have gotten "Everything's Coming Up Moses."

BORN ON THE FOURTH OF JULY. Crippled Vietnam War veteran played by Tom Cruise comes home embittered and emotionally scarred. He upsets his devoutly Catholic mother by yelling naughty words at her.

THORN BIRDS. Handsome young priest is tempted in the desert of the Australian outback and succumbs. Notable chiefly as the made-for-TV movie that established Richard Chamberlain as a fixture in all subsequent major miniseries.

THE GODFATHER. Gripping story of Italian immigrant family who make it big as mobsters. Highlight is the si-multaneous murder of five rival capos during the Baptism of young Michael Corleone's son.

THE GODFATHER PART II. Not letting a little murder, drugs and prostitution stand between them and their Catholic faith, the Corleones throw the Godmother of all First Communion parties for little Anthony. Soon after, Michael has his brother Fredo killed while Fredo is praying the Hail Mary.

THE GODFATHER PART III. Michael Corleone, the worst guy in the world, lucks out by getting the kindest priest in the world the one time he goes to Confession.

MY LEFT FOOT. Should have been called *My Right Arm*, which is what Christy Brown's mother, a good Irish Catholic lady with twenty-three children, would have given for permission to use birth control.

CHURCH LATIN
It's All Greek to Me

Before Vatican II, the Mass was said in Latin. For many centuries, the priest did all the talking, but eventually the congregation got to chime in as well. Since Latin was a language that very few of them understood, the only way the could do this was to learn their set responses phonetically, the way the Miss Universe contestants from many countries would learn the English words to the poignant pageant theme song. The resulting utterances—during both contest and Mass—were similarly odd-sounding.

True, the Church did provide Latin-English missals so that the Faithful would know what they and the priest were saying. These ecclesiastical Berlitz guides were of little practical use, however, since the priest usually spoke so rapidly, so softly, and with such a bad accent that one couldn't tell exactly where he was. It didn't help that his back was to the congregation most of the time as he faced the altar.

The Mass in translation, like many a subtitled foreign movie, was hard to follow. Only a few phrases from the Latin Mass really penetrated the consciousness of most Catholics, usually for all the wrong reasons. The following is a list of these select phrases, why we remember them, and what their real meaning to us was.

"In nomine Patris, et Filii, et Spiritus Sancti."

> Translation: "In the name of the Father, and of the Son, and of the Holy Spirit."

This was the kickoff, the very first thing the priest said, and so only a few members of the congregation had gotten lost by this point, or were there to hear it.

"Sicut erat in principio, et nunc, et semper: et in saecula saeculorum. Amen."

> "As it was in the beginning, is now and ever shall be: world without end. Amen."

This phrase punctuated the Mass periodically, providing a familiar signpost amid all the unfamiliar verbiage. Like the occasional Howard Johnson's restaurant along a bleak stretch of interstate highway, it meant progress was being made, however tediously. Amen. The *"in saecula saeculorum"* part was particularly memorable because of the alliteration.

"In nomine Domini."
"In the name of the Lord."

Another phrase to delight the ear. Rhyming words always made things much easier.

"Confiteor Deo omnipotenti . . ."
"I confess to almight God . . ."

The Latin Mass might be compared to a business meeting. After a bit of chitchat and a series of respectful introductions, it was time to get down to the nitty-gritty, and of course the first item on the agenda was Our Sins. The Confiteor is a long sequence. It is the original "litany of errors."

"Mea culpa, mea culpa, mea maxima culpa."
"Through my fault, through my fault, through my most grievous fault."

This was the culmination of the Confiteor, where everyone got to strike his breast three times on the strong beat. It is also a perfect illustration of the real reason why Catholics have so much guilt: because the Church made it all seem so glamorous. Those who doubt this should take note of the following rapturous excerpt from a Missal used in the 1950s: "A dramatic picture indeed! humbly striking our breast, symbol of stirring up conscience, of disciplining body and soul; first confessing our sins publicly, then beseeching grace and help from God, the Church in heaven and on earth."

"Misereatur vestri omnipotens Deus . . ."
"May almight God have mercy upon you . . ."

It was the part that sounded like "misery" that caught the ear, since this was what you were often feeling by this point. The bonus was that you felt you were doing Penance merely by attending, as well as fulfilling the weekly Obligation.

"Gloria in Excelsis Deo."
"Glory to God in the Highest."

You knew this one because it was the refrain to the lovely Christmas hymn of the same name, also known as "Angels We Have Heard on High."

"Kyrie Eleison."
"Lord, have mercy."

Not Latin at all, but Greek. The beginning of a very moving chant. This became the title of a rock-and-roll hymn sung by the Byrds in the 1960s, used in the soundtrack of the film *Easy Rider*. A song called "Kyrie" by the band Mr. Mister became a hit in 1986.

NAME THAT HYMN

A. "And humbly I'll receive Thee, the Bridegroom of my soul"
B. "Sweet Sacrament! We Thee adore. Oh make us love Thee more and more"
C. *"Fit panis hominum: Dat panis coelicus!"*
D. "Near thee, Madonna, fondly we hover"
E. "Our hearts are on fire"
F. "O Mary we crown Thee with blossoms today"
G. *"O piissima"*
H. *"Quae coeli pandis hostium"*
I. *"Veneremur cernui"*
J. *"Gló-ó-o-o-o-ó-ó-o-o-o-ó-ó-o-o-o-ó-ria, in excelsis Deo"*
K. "Milk and honey on the other side"

1. On This Day, O Beautiful Mother
2. O Lord, I Am Not Worthy
3. *O Salutaris Hostia*
4. Angels We Have Heard on High
5. *O Sanctissima*
6. Jesus, My Lord, My God, My All
7. Michael, Row Your Boat Ashore
8. Immaculate Mary
9. *Tantum Ergo*
10. *Panis Angelicus*
11. Bring Flowers of the Rarest

MY FIRST HYMNAL
FAVORITE CATHOLIC HYMNS
arranged
FOR PIANO
by
ADA RICHTER

"Dominus vobiscum."

"Et cum spiritu tuo."

"Oremus."
"The Lord be with you."
"And with your spirit."
"Let us pray."

This was the most familiar set piece of the entire Mass, repeated again and again. We wondered how many times we had to be reminded the Lord was with us. Once He arrived, wouldn't He stay for a while? *"Et cum spiritu tuo," contrary to popular belief, was not the rectory phone number.* "Oremus" meant "Here we go again."

"Sanctus, sanctus, sanctus . . ."
"Holy, holy, holy . . ."

The lovely repetition got 'em every time.

"Per Christum Dominum Nostrum."
"Through Christ Our Lord."

A lot of "ums."

"Per Ipsum, et Cum Ipso, et In Ipso."
"Through Him, with Him, and in Him."

A real Latin tongue twister.

"Ite, Missa est."
"Deo gratias."
"Go, the Mass is ended."
"Thanks be to God."

You said it. *"Deo gratias"* gets by far the heartiest response of the day.

OUR PARENT, WHO ART IN HEAVEN:
How to Be Liturgically Correct

A religious version of Political Correctness is gaining ground among many Catholics. They want to be Liturgically Correct, or L.C. One goal of the L.C. movement is to eliminate sexist language from Catholic prayers and rituals. Another is to make the meanings of these prayers and rituals more clear by expressing them in modern language.

There are a few basic realities in this L.C. business that can't be ignored. After all, Jesus was a man. He sometimes referred to God as His Father. And the greatest mysteries of human existence are best expressed in rich poetic imagery, not flat, overly literal L.C. prose. But there's no reason to cling to outdated or highfalutin' language for its own sake.

There are some who think that the Vatican has already gone quite far enough by allowing U.S. Catholics to drop "men" from the phrase "who died for us and for all men" in the Creed. On the other side, there are those who won't be happy until every "He" and "Him" is changed to "God" in every ancient hymn (hyrm?).

The following list of terms should be helpful to Catholics who want to be as L.C. as possible:

Non-L.C.	L.C.
Mankind	Humanity; all
Brothers	Brothers and sisters
Father	Parent
Son	Child
He	God; the One
Him	God
Lord	God; Holy One
Christ	God; Jesus
His	God's
Thy	Your
Thine	Yours

GONNA TAKE A MIRACLE:
How Saints Are Made

The Christian Church has been venerating saints ever since the second century. For the early saints, there was no formal canonization process—they simply became saints by popular acclaim. And potential saints who pull in the crowds continue to be stronger possibilities for sainthood than holy nobodies. But for the past thousand years or so, saints have been formally chosen by the Sacred Congregation for the Causes of Saints, commonly known as "the saint factory."

Vatican II reforms pruned a Church calendar that was bursting with saints. But Pope John Paul II has more than made up for these recalls of early saints by becoming the biggest saint-maker in history. He has canonized 260 of the 700 official saints that have been recorded since the tenth century.

The Church is looking to broaden its cadre of saints, to seek out worthy Catholics who aren't part of the European white male contingent that makes up over half the saint roster. Since most saints are priests, bishops, and nuns, an effort is being made to canonize more "regular folks" as well. Furthermore, potential saints are being searched out in lands just coming back into the fold of the faithful, such as the Eastern European countries. Perhaps not entirely by coincidence, there are great numbers of Poles on the docket, and these candidates are moving through the process with unusual alacrity. One potential saint whose controversial candidacy is progressing with extraordinary speed is that of Father Josemaría Escriva, the Spanish priest who founded Opus Dei, the ultraconservative Catholic organization.

The always-mysterious saint-making process has certainly come a long way over the years. In 1985 the saint-makers' office acquired its first two photocopy machines. Computers are now used, and documents no longer have to be handwritten in Latin. The prosecuting counsel, popularly known as the Devil's Advocate, has been eliminated from the proceedings.

Currently, there are more than 2,000 candidates for sainthood waiting for the nod. Their supporters bide their time as they try to meet the toughest requirement of all—proof of two miracles. Both miracles must occur after the candidate's death—one before beatification and one before canonization. But long before candidates get to that point, another miracle of a financial nature must take place, since the cost of promoting the average modern-day canonization is now in the neighborhood of $250,000.

THE DEVIL'S ADVOCATE:
Certifying Sainthood

It was three o'clock in the morning on a Sunday and I was sitting in my shabby little office in the Vatican, sipping some leftover Communion wine and puffing on the last of my Luckies. I thought I saw a shadow pass by the smoky glass of my cracked office window, the one with the barely legible stencil, FR. SAM GUMSHOE, D.A. I kicked back my chair and took a few tentative steps toward the door. A stillness had fallen over this back corridor in the bowels of the Holy City, but then again things are always pretty quiet in this part of the Vatican— we call it the Catacombs.

I reached silently for a crozier that was propped up against the wall. (Some bozo cardinal from Wagangi left it here and I never got around to shipping it back to him. God knows where Wagangi is.) Slowly the door began to open with an ominous squeak. As I hefted the crozier, the shadow crept into my dimly lit, dank-smelling office like an uninvited guest at a cocktail party.

The door, now fully opened, revealed the outline of a man, but the hall lights blaring eerily and incessantly behind the figure made it nearly impossible to see who it was. But then, that unmistakable twinkle of the eye that I had come to know and love shot forth from the apparition's countenance and allayed my growing fears. "Oh, it's you, Your Holiness!" I gasped, lowering the crozier, which now seemed silly in my hand. "Yes, my son," he said in his pontifical manner. For indeed it was him, the man who signed our paychecks, the man we affectionately called the Jeep—John Paul II. The Holy Father.

"Your Holiness," I said. That's what I called him, Your Holiness. "Your Holiness, what brings you down these hallowed halls at this time of night?" He smiled benignly and pulled up a chair. "What are you working on, my son?" "Well, Father"—I called him Father sometimes too—"I'm looking to close the file on the tortilla thing over in the States." He knew all too well that I meant the recent claims by a pious woman in New Mexico that she had seen the face of Our Lord in a tortilla she was making. There had

been some doubt cast upon her account when it was discovered that she was actually making a burrito at the time. "And then I want to check into this sighting in Montana."

He smiled benignly again and said, "Go easy on them, my son, for they have not many saints and yet have many who follow the way." With a small wave and a quick blessing he exited the office just as quickly as he had come. I returned to my cluttered desk, pushed aside the dusty files so I could put up my well-worn black shoes, and clicked off the lamp. I sat in the dark for a while. I knew His Holiness meant well, but damnit, I was a professional, and it was my job to be tough. You see, I'm the Devil's Advocate.

It is one of the toughest, dirtiest jobs in the Vatican. I investigate the claims to sainthood, and with my recent transfer to UHO (Unidentified Holy Observations) I check out reported sightings of the Big Four on earth. Although the Trinity generally is pretty easy to verify, sightings of Mary can be a lot tougher. Let's face it, it's my job to prove these things *don't* happen, not that they *do*. You don't make a whole bunch of friends at this end of the Vatican.

That's why I'm opening my notebook on the investigation of the now-famous "Mary in Montana" sightings. The job of the Devil's Advocate is complex and important. The certification of a saint can take years, even centuries—in fact, usually centuries—and the paperwork is unbelievable. Since almost anyone who can be proven to have seen Our Lady has a shot at sainthood, we have to start investigating these cases from the beginning. What follows are my notes from the "Mary in Montana" case. In the beginning, there was the word from Bozeman, Montana, and before I knew it I was winging my way across the Atlantic on the Papal jet, *Wings of the Dove.*

Excerpts from the Notebook of a Devil's Advocate

Cruising my way across the uncharted wastelands of Montana in my rented Chevette, I reflected on my mission. It wasn't going to be my job to figure out whether the Mother of God had actually been seen in a cow pasture south of Bozeman; that was already under investigation. I had been sent to check on an application for sainthood made by a parish priest on behalf of the little child who claimed to have had the visions, and to determine if this saintly little girl was actually a candidate for one of the most exclusive clubs in the universe.

The "Little One of Bozeman," as she was called, was recently deceased and the Chief wanted me to start compiling a file on her right away, instead of waiting for centuries as we usually do. We agreed to do the legwork at the site instead of flying witnesses to the Vatican, since air fare had been causing havoc in accounting lately.

I was told I could find the "Little One's" father at a beer-and-shot joint called the Watch Where You Step. He was a grizzled but honest-looking man of about fifty. I sidled up to him and stated my business. "You from the papers?" he said, eyeing me suspiciously. "No, no, my son," I reassured him, "from the Holy See." He stared, uncomprehending. "The Vatican," I added. "Got any ID?" he asked, knocking back what must have been one of many that after-noon. I flashed him my Devil's Advocate Badge and it seemed to calm him down. "Just the facts," I said in my most businesslike tone.

Based on an extensive interview with the father of the "Little One of Bozeman," the following notes should be checked:

- "Little One of Bozeman," born Elizabeth Mae Dirsack in Bozeman. Age at decease, 9 years.
- Claimed to have seen a "beautiful lady" in Morris Cow Pasture, May 22.
- Claimed lady told her not to go to school, but to come back to the pasture "sometime next month."
- A large crowd gathered when Elizabeth Mae returned to the pasture on June 17.
- It rained on a crowd of about twenty who accompanied the small girl.
- A man with a huge goiter was said to be instantly cured.
- The sun came out when it stopped raining.
- Elizabeth claimed that the lady told her to continue to avoid school and attend movies at every opportunity.

RECOMMENDATIONS:

Not only do I think that there should be no recommendation for veneration, beatification, or canonization, but I think they ought to lock this bunch of loonies up. As it turns out, the so-called "Little One" was not deceased, as was first reported. She had been attending a continuous weekend feature at the Bijou. The miraculous cure of the goiter was actually a minor relief of a chronic case of gout. The father, when sober, revealed that he isn't even a Catholic. The "Little One" apparently was suspended from school and made up this whole idiotic story so she wouldn't have to tell her parents.

CONCLUSION:
APPLICATION DENIED. REPRIMAND IN ORDER FOR LOCAL PRIEST.

CLIMBING THE STAIRWAY TO HEAVEN
Steps to Sainthood

- A saint must have practiced more than "common sanctity."
- A saint must have all the virtues to a "heroic" degree.
- A saint must be more than "mediocre in a nice way."
- A saint must practice mortification. Self-torture, however, is not allowable.
- A saint must reach religious perfection and this must be apparent to all around him.
- A saint must be responsible for miracles through his or her intercession.
- A saint must be venerated by the Faithful.

- A saint must be investigated by the Church through the "Devil's Advocate." This formal process has a zillion steps and takes forever.
- A saint must be "beatified" before becoming a saint. This allows the saint to be shown "religious honors."
- After enough time has passed and the record checks out, the "beatified" can be made a "saint." Holy cards are then prepared for worldwide distribution.

MR. CHRISTOPHER:
The Un-Saint

There was recently a nasty piece of news circulating that caused many good Catholics and a number of sacred medal-makers quite a bit of distress. The story was that St. Christopher, the beloved patron saint of travel, had been demoted. Needless to say, this didn't sit too well with the millions who had worn their medals to the nub by fingering them religiously on airplane flights, or when getting a ride from Sister to the bake sale.

The problem developed when it was discovered that St. Christopher was not just one person but a composite of several ancient martyrs. But it's not fair that faulty scholarship

on the part of the Church should be held against the guy we have come to know and love as St. Christopher. That guy, of course, was the one who was sitting by the river, probably fishing or doing some other saintly thing, when a little baby came up and tried to get across the river, which began getting a little choppy as soon as the kid started across. Christopher saw the kid in trouble, hoisted him up on his shoulders, and got him to the other side where he discovered the child was really Baby Jesus, who had not yet learned to walk on water. Nice story, and besides, if St. Christopher is demoted, who is going to be the patron saint of travel?*

We suggest that until this whole thing is worked out, it might be better to refer to our bearded, beloved "Good Samaritan" as Mr. Christo-

---

*Actually, there are several other contenders. St. Anthony of Padua, St. Nicholas of Myra, and St. Raphael are also legitimate patron saints of travel. There is even a patron saint of travel hostesses—St. Bona—apparently the result of lobbying by the airline industry in 1962. There is not yet a patron saint of People Express, although Patience has been suggested.

pher. Those wishing to join the fight to keep Mr. Christopher from remaining an unsaint might think about starting Christopher clubs to write nice but pointed letters to the powers-that-be. They can be reached at St. Peter's, Vatican City.

AN UNOFFICIAL WHO'S WHO OF POPES

St. Peter the Apostle was the first, and 301 popes later (including antipopes), John Paul II became the latest in line. Who were these remarkable men? Here's a little background on some of our more colorful Church leaders.

Fabian (236–50). Great name. Pretty great Pope too, from the sketchy details known of his life. He is most remembered for the way in which he was selected to be Pope. According to Eusebius, a later Pope, a dove landed on Fabian's head as the clergy were mulling over names. Even though no one had considered Fabian a candidate, he got the job. Who's to argue with the Holy Spirit?

Martin I (649–53). Martin was known for his independent spirit, which got him into trouble when he had himself consecrated without getting the permission of the Holy Roman Emperor, who then refused to recognize him as Pope. Martin ignored the rebuff, so the emperor had him arrested, deposed, and shipped off to Constantinople to live out his last years in solitary confinement. He resigned himself to his fate and prayed until he died from cold, starvation, and harsh treatment. It was not long before the Church came to venerate him as a martyr.

Stephen (II) (752). Stephen (II), as he is commonly known, was elected and installed as Pope in 752. He had a stroke three days after the election and died the following day. He is perhaps best known for messing up the numberings of popes with the same name, who are usually referred to as Stephen II (III), Steven III (IV), Stephen IV (V), and so on.

Formosus (891–96). Formosus didn't have many enemies, but one of them was his successor, Stephen VI (VII), who had extremely bizarre ideas about turning the other cheek. Nine months after Formosus' death, Stephen had the body exhumed and propped up on a throne in full pontifical vestments. Stephen went on to preside over a mock trial, in which (surprise!) Formosus was found guilty of perjury, of having coveted the papal throne, and of a few other infractions. Stephen declared all his predecessor's acts and ordinations to be null and void, and tossed Formosus' body into the Tiber River. A hermit found it. Soon there were reports of miracles worked by the mutilated corpse. The following year, a friendlier Pope ordered Formosus to be reburied in his original grave in St. Peter's.

John XII (955–64). Just eighteen when elected, John kept Roman tongues wagging with his disinterest in the spiritual life and his fondness for boor-ish pleasures. Gossip that this bad-boy Pope was turning the papal palace into a brothel was given credence when he had a stroke, allegedly while in bed with a married woman. He died a week later, still only in his mid-twenties.

Celestine IV (1294–96). After two years without a Pope, feuding cardinals heard that a devout hermit had prophesied heavenly retribution if the Church went without a leader much longer. In the hope that a bold stroke would rejuvenate the papacy, they elected the hermit, who accepted under extreme duress. Celestine was eighty-five years old when elected, the eleventh child of Italian peasants. As a teenager, he entered a Benedictine monastery, but was drawn to the solitary life and lived by himself in a cave for many years. He seemed not to like being Pope, and wanted to hand over the papacy to a few cardinals so he could fast and pray. This offer was rejected. Stripping off his papal insignia and begging to be allowed to return to his cave, Celestine was detained under guard. He escaped for several months, but was captured and locked in a castle tower until his death.

John XXI (1276–77). Many Popes throughout history were writers, but John is probably the only Pope who wrote a published work on ophthalmology, called *The Eye.* As irritating to papal list makers as Stephen (II), he bungled the numberings for Johns when—oops—he forgot that there was no XX and called himself XXI. John died an untimely death when the ceiling of his study collapsed on him.

Urban VI (1378–89). Urban was elected amidst a swirl of French-Roman competition for popehood. Crowds demonstrated in the streets of Rome, begging for a Roman, or at least an Italian, as the next Pope. In a panic-stricken session, the cardinals acqui-

esced and voted for Urban. No one knew about his stubbornness, violent recalcitrance, and general mental instability. After being pushed to their limits by the Pope's uncontrollable tirades, the cardinals met secretly. Urban rejected their "invitation" to abdicate, and at that point, the cardinals informed the world that he had been deposed. They elected a new Pope, Clement VII, which brought about what is known as the Great Schism. Urban and Clement, after officially excommunicating one another, spent their days sending out letters all over Europe in which each claimed to be the true Pope. A war ensued, along with much plotting, intrigue, tortured cardinals, poisonings, and the like.

Leo X (1513–21). This spend-thrift was a Renaissance man who loved nothing more than to patronize the arts. But he also had wars and crusades to pay for. On top of that, the construction of St. Peter's was costing a bundle. Unfortunately for the financially strapped Pope, parish bazaars had not yet been invented. He pawned the palace furniture, borrowed extensively, sold cardinalships and other offices, and renewed the selling of indulgences. Leo died suddenly of malaria, leaving the papal treasury deeply in debt.

John Paul I (1978). He remarked that he might have become a journalist if he had not become a priest. He wrote a collection of fanciful but incisive letters to authors and characters in history and fiction, including Pinocchio and Figaro. He chose his papal name in a desire to combine the progressive and traditional qualities of the two previous Popes. After his election, he held a spontaneous press conference, where he enraptured thousands of journalists. John Paul's reign was cut short by an untimely heart attack after he had been in office only three weeks. Rumors of foul play followed, incited by a report that he was poisoned because of his plan to clean up the Vatican Bank, but these rumors were never substantiated.

IX

Quo Vadis?*

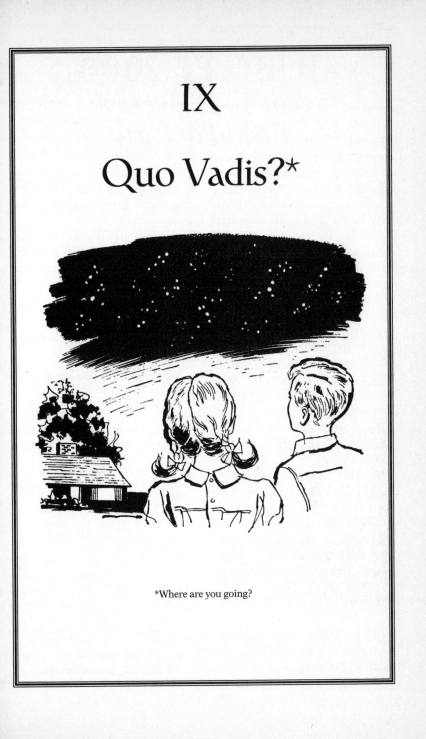

*Where are you going?

JUBILEE 2000
Not Your Average Birthday Party

The Catholic Church is celebrating a year-long birthday bash, and you're invited! There'll be plenary indulgences-made-easy (you don't have to go to the Vatican anymore—a stop at the airport chapel in Rome gets the job done). Forgiveness of debt (not yours). Rejoicing and repenting (in that order). Pilgrimages (to Rome, Jerusalem or, for reluctant travelers, your local cathedral). And let's not forget the rest. Vigils. Prayer. Fasting. This is sounding less fun by the minute. But who ever said the Catholic Church was about fun? Hey, this isn't Jamboree 2000. The Boy Scouts are having that one.

Catholics in the United States have been called upon to pledge themselves to Eight Good Things, in addition to the Ten Good Things we already try to observe. They are:

- Pray for justice and peace
- Learn about Catholic social teaching
- Reach across boundaries of religion, race, ethnicity, gender and disabling conditions
- Live justly in family life, school, work, the marketplace and the political arena

WHOSE MILLENNIUM IS IT ANYWAY?

Memorial Day is the last Monday of May, Father's Day is the third Sunday in June, and Arbor Day is the first of September. It doesn't matter to the calendar whether you're a veteran, or a dad, or a tree. Likewise, the year A.D. 2000 marks the two thousandth anniversary (more or less) of the birth of Christ, whether you are a Christian or not. (That's what A.D. stands for: Anno Domini, the year of Our Lord.)

There are other ways of counting. In the Hebrew calendar, it's 5760, not 2000. According to the Chinese lunar calendar, it's 4698, the year of the dragon. In the Islamic tradition, it's 1420. But the Gregorian calendar starts with the Big Bang in Bethlehem.

- Serve the poor and vulnerable
- Give generously to those in need
- Advocate beneficial public policies
- Encourage others to work for charity, justice and peace

There might be a familiar ring to many of these pledges. Remember the Corporal and Spiritual Works of Mercy? But that would sound impossibly old-fashioned today, so here they are again, dressed up in party clothes.

YOU KNOW ECUMENISM HAS GONE TOO FAR WHEN . . .

1. Nobody says Merry Christmas anymore. It's Happy Holidays now.
2. Catholics can't decide who to listen to, their parish priest or the Dalai Lama.
3. Married Episcopal priests become Catholic, and bring their children to live in the rectory.
4. Perfectly ordinary Catholics start speaking in tongues.
5. Catholics baptize by dunking, just like the Baptists.
6. Martin Luther would have to hang only 76 Theses today because treaties between Catholics and Lutherans have resolved 20 contested issues.
7. Rudolph the Red-Nosed Reindeer has menorah antlers on a Christmas/Hanukkah card.
8. Communion is a "come one, come all" affair, like an open bar at a wedding.
9. Muslim fasting rules are tougher than Catholic ones.
10. Following Vatican City's lead, Jerry Falwell declares Lynchburg, Virginia, an independent country and starts issuing postage stamps.

THE NAME GAME

As Holy Mother Church approaches a new millennium, the marketing department at the Vatican has been working overtime to develop a new look for her. Although changing the color of the Cardinals' vestments from red to blue (and calling them the Blue Jays instead) didn't get papal approval, His Holiness did give the go-ahead for a contest to find a catchier and more timely name for the One, Holy, Catholic and Apostolic Church. Here are some of the early entries:

RC Worldwide
The Big Church
Rome One
The Catholic Group
iVatican.com
Heaven Direct
ePray
Rome Depot

In a related move, Vatican officials announced a search for a slogan to spearhead their planned advertising campaign. Some slogans under consideration are:

The Official Church of the New Millennium
Work Hard, Die Right
Just Don't Do It
The World Serious
The Popesi Generation
Got God?
This Old House (of God)
Goys 'R' Us
It's Your Soul, Stupid
The Only Church You'll Ever Need
Hell, No!
It Takes a Vatican
There's No Church Like Rome
It's Not Just About Hell Anymore
2,000 More Years, 20,000 More Years, 200,000 More Years

THINGS WE EXPECT THE ROMAN CATHOLIC CHURCH TO DO IN THE NEW MILLENNIUM

1. Allow priests and nuns to get married (but only to each other).
2. Instead of twelve Our Fathers or twelve Hail Marys, have priests give a twelve-step program to penitents so they won't have to listen to the same sins over and over and over again.
3. Project papal election results based on exit polls from the College of Cardinals.
4. Alternate men popes with women popes.
5. Make priestly vestments in blueberry, tangerine, grape and other iMac colors.
6. End the debate over homosexuality and call gays "Particularly Happy Catholics."
7. Have a Vatican III to clear up any confusion over Vatican II.
8. Elect an Italian pope.

WWW.HOLY.COM

Now that the Vatican has its own website, the Pope has his own calling card, and lots of beatific screen savers are available for those whose salvation comes by way of the laptop, here are some other high-tech tie-ins we expect the Church to consider in the next few years:

VOICE RECOGNITION CONFESSION

Log on to a special site by way of modem. The computer bank will recognize your voice and print out a list of past sins so the cyber-confessor has a complete profile before giving penance and absolution.

HIGH-SPEED INTERNET MASS

Downloads in seven minutes as opposed to the fifty minutes a traditional Mass usually takes. High Mass downloads take slightly longer.

VATICAN.COM TWO-CHANNEL DIGITAL CALLING

Adds new meaning to song lyrics like "Jesus is on the mainline/Call him up," and allows you to have heavenly conversations in both analog and cell sectors of the world. Lovely Papal logo in gold foil and white on each compact digital phone.

PRE-PAID INDULGENCES CARD

Special Catholic Edition pre-paid indulgence card has 250,000 years of indulgences which you can swipe at special ATMs in churches around the world.

AUTOMOBILE ST. LORAN LOCATOR

Similar to the electronic mapping systems, this handy device locates the closest Catholic church or hospital, with directions.

PALM PONTIFF V

Handheld device with all the ex-cathedra papal rulings (and more, including the newly released Vatican secret files!) to consult anytime, anywhere.

BALTIMORE CATECHISM 6.0

New software for children modeled on the "Who Wants to Be a Millionaire?" format; the questions get harder as you get closer to "Heaven."

ANSUBSTANTIATION-TRAY:
Can't Anybody Here Speak Latin Anymore?

Efore-bay atican-Vay II, the oman-Ray atholic-Cay ass-May as-way aid-say in-yay atin-Lay. Erever-whay ou-yay ent-way in-yay the orld-way, ou-yay ot-gay the ame-say ass-May—ust-jay ike-lay icDonald's-May, ere-why ou-yay et-gay the ame-say urger-bay and ies-fray in-yay aris-Pay, ance-Fray, as ou-yay et-gay in-yay aris-Pay, exas-Tay. We ealize-ray eye-why ope-Pay ohn-Jay XXIII ecided-day at-thay ass-May in-yay the ernacular-vay—in-yay our-yay own anguage-lay, at-thay is—as-way an ood-gay idea-yay. It-yay ade-may the ass-May easier oo-tay ollow-fay. Evertheless-nay, we iked-lay atin-Lay ass-May, and we ew-knay at-whay it-yay eant-may, ecause-bay the uns-nay aught-tay us. Ow-nay it's in-yay our other-may ongue-tay, ut-bay it-yay oesn't-day ound-say as eautiful-bay anymore.

O-say e're-way oposing-pray an ompromise-cay: ay-say the ass-May in ig-Pay atin-Lay. At-thay ould-way ive-gay us the est-bay of oth-bay orlds-way, i.e. (ee-say? it's eally-ray ool-cay), an anguage-lay at-thay as-hay an odicum-may of ystery-may, ut-bay is omprehended-cay all over the orld-way. Ère-fray acques-Jay. Éliz-fay avidad-Nay. Ao-ciay.

WHO WILL BE THE NEXT CATHOLIC PRESIDENT?

Andrew Cuomo

*Arnold
Schwarzenegger*

Jeb Bush

Rudolph Giuliani

WHO WILL BE THE NEXT POPE?:
A Handicapper's Take

ITALIANS

Dionigi Cardinal Tettamanzi, Archbishop of Genoa.
Morning Line: Who doesn't like salami? This veteran Italian-bred is ripe for a big win. 3–1.

Angelo Cardinal Soldano, Papal Secretary of State.
Morning Line: Been training for this ultimate stake for a long time. Fit with lots of breeding and wins under his belt. Can go sprints or 1 mile and a quarter. A real thoroughbred. This front-runner could wire this field from an excellent post position. Should go off as the favorite at 2–1.

Carlo Cardinal Martini, Archbishop of Milan. A Jesuit and one of the most liberal members of the Sacred College.
Morning Line: Winner of three stakes as a juvenile, but the extra distances of big stakes races cause him to fade in the stretch. Should have stayed at home. 100–1.

EUROPEANS

Christoph Cardinal Schönborn, O.P., Archbishop of Vienna. Member of an ancient Austrian family of the Holy Roman Empire; brilliant theologian who helped write the Catechism.
Morning Line: A solid horse in this field but may get stuck in the middle of the pack if he doesn't break well. 5–1.

Jean Marie Cardinal Lustiger, Archbishop of Paris. A convert from Judaism.
Morning Line: This old campaigner has outsmarted a good field before but this distance may take its toll. 20–1.

SOUTH AMERICANS

Darío Cardinal Castrillón Hoyos, a Colombian and currently head of the Congregation for the Clergy; he wired most of the Colombian Church for the computer age.

Morning Line: This good-looking colt could cause trouble for the field as he trains well for a bow in Rome. Handlers are using high-tech training methods to bring him to form. 15–1.

Lucas Cardinal Moreira Neves, O.P. Former archbishop of São Salvador da Bahia Brazil, and currently the head of the powerful Congregation of Bishops. He was the Pope's Brazilian antidote to the arch-liberal Aloisio Cardinal Lorscheider, O.F.M.

Morning Line: A gamer but may find this company a little too much. Shipping in will tire him and he will need another race to get into form. 50–1.

AFRICANS

Francis Cardinal Arinze. Former Archbishop of Onitsha, Nigeria, currently the head of the Pontifical Council for Interreligious Dialogue; responsible for the recent great relations between the Church and Muslims; plays a mean game of tennis.

Morning Line: We may be the world but it would take a world-class effort to beat this field from a far outside post position. 70–1.

DARK HORSE

Francis Cardinal George, Archbishop of Chicago.

Morning Line: He may be no Joe Bernardin but this brainy Chicago home-bred has lots of heart and is especially dangerous down the stretch if the front runners tire. 50–1.

BEWARE THE HORSE NO ONE LOOKS AT

Morning Line: Keep your eye on Archbishop Jean Louis Tauran of the Secretariat of State. Who hasn't heard of Secretariat? This son of the great one is rumored to ship in just for this stakes. 3–1 if he posts.

HOW WE'RE DOING:
Catholic Facts and Figures

The 2000 Catholic Almanac reported that in 1999:

THE GOOD NEWS

- There were 62,018,436 Catholics in the United States, 454,667 more than the previous year.
- Permanent deacons rose in number to 12,675, which is 428 more than the year before and more than double the number of a decade ago.
- The number of Baptisms or initiations of baptized Christians from other denominations stood at 1,184,828.
- Approximately 2.3 million U.S. Catholics are African-American.
- There were 19,584 parishes; 3,316,143 students in Catholic elementary schools, high schools and colleges; 626,570 Confirmations; and 878,431 First Holy Communions.

THE BAD NEWS

- The number of priests stood at 47,199, down 364 from the previous year.
- The number of priestly ordinations decreased to 478 from 509 the previous year.
- The number of nuns was 85,034, which reflects a loss of more than 1,378 in the past year.
- Religious brothers numbered 5,970, dropping from 6,115.
- Only about 273,700 Catholic marriages were performed, down approximately 20 percent in the past five years.

LETTER TO GOD FROM AN OLD PRIEST

Dear God,

I have just finished taking a short walk in the garden behind St. Stephen's Church, where I was reflecting on my last sixty years as a parish priest. Before I leave this place, there are a few things I have to say to you.

Thank you for my time in the confessional waiting for the sliding shutter to open, reading my morning paper, and hearing the breathy, guilty whisper of one of our parishioners. (I knew everyone's voice after a few years.)

Thank you for the rustling of Sister Marguerite's skirts as she stepped from darkened classroom to darkened classroom, making sure all was in order.

Thank you for the smell of incense from the censer on Corpus Christi; the little chains on it sounded like the chirping of small birds.

Thank you for the scared but beatific little boys who handed me the water cruet when I wanted the wine and the wine when I wanted the water.

Thank you for the handful of saintly old ladies who came to church every day for 7 A.M. Mass.

Thank you for a church full of families who kindly left gifts, usually booze, on the rectory steps.

Thank you for the sight and sound of lines of unruly children being marched into class, for the joyous noises of recess, for the thump of the handball against the rectory wall.

Thank you for the exquisite weight of the vestments on my shoulders.

Thank you for St. Teresa of Ávila and Teilhard de Chardin, whom I read in the evenings while the altar linens were being pressed by the nuns in the convent next door.

The light in St. Stephen's and in my heart is bright as I prepare to leave.

See you soon.

NUN-PAREIL

When Susan Sarandon won an Oscar for her portrayal of the real-life Sister Helen Prejean in *Dead Man Walking*, it was a victory not just for a brilliant actress, but for nuns everywhere. Sarandon had finally done what no one else seemed to get quite right before: she captured the spirit of the modern nun at her very best.

Nuns have come in for a lot of ribbing over the years from their former charges, including the authors of this book. Underneath the caricature of nun-as-drill-sergeant, there was always affection, but many of today's nuns understandably chafe at the stereotype. Like Sister Helen, they have taken seriously the call of Vatican II to become involved with the contemporary world. In their street clothes, they may look much like other professional women. But today's nuns are expected to do much more than perform good works, important as those may be. They are called to "be the presence of God for you," as Sarandon says in the film. And they model this behavior for the rest of us Catholics, who of course are called to do nothing less.

Sarandon, a former Catholic schoolgirl, put in years of research for her role. She did not waste them, as is evident not just on the screen but in her real-life commitment to a number of social causes. Sarandon's high school nuns undoubtedly would have raised their eyebrows about the fact that she and her life partner, actor-director Tim Robbins, live together and are raising children "without the benefit of matrimony," as the phrase used to go. But they would otherwise be very proud of what she has done with her work and her life, and confident that their lessons had not been lost on her.

DON'T EVEN GO THERE:
Father Phil, Confessor to the Sopranos

He's handsome, smart and looks great in black. He's got traditional values. He loves movies—especially *Casablanca* (sigh) and *The Remains of the Day* (smoldering passion). He likes quiet nights at home in front of the fire with a glass of Chianti or Lillet. He's a great listener. Caring. Forgiving. He has a great appetite; he's a pleasure to feed.

Sounds like the perfect date, doesn't he? Well, he's not. He's Father Phil. Too bad for Carmela Soprano. Like generations of Catholic women before her, Carmela is in love with her priest. Who else can she talk to so trustingly? What other man wants to spend so much time with her? Who the hell loves her ziti like he does? Innocent enough, if it stopped there. But since this is the twenty-first century, the harmless fantasy of millions of Catholic girls and women can now—at least on this show—be a little more fully realized. Father Phil should know better. It's one thing to eat over and watch movies on a hot DVD; it's one thing to counsel Carmela on her marriage; it's one thing to carry a little torch for one of his parishioners. But Communion by firelight? Don't even go there! And besides, she's the don's wife. Is he crazy or what? How long can she fend Tony off by telling him that Father Phil, her "spiritual mentor," is "helping her to be a better Catholic"? Tony may be dumb, but he's not stupid. He knows they're not playing Name That Pope. This is like the plot of an opera. No wonder they call it *The Sopranos*. If Father Phil doesn't watch out, he'll end up as Father Castrato.

ARE YOU SEARCHING FOR THE ANSWER?

Millions of people around the world have seen a kind of mystical significance in the number 2000, aside from the fact that it marks one of Christ's really major birthdays. Indeed, numbers play an important role in Catholicism, offering us many spiritual guideposts. Think of the number 3, for example. We dug into scripture and tradition to come up with other significant numbers, feeling sure that they would yield enlightenment. As we looked at the list, we realized that the answer was staring us right in the face:

```
  The 10  Commandments
+ The 12  Apostles
+ The  5  Decades of the
          Rosary
+ The 12  Days of Christmas
+ The  8  Beatitudes
+ The  5  Sorrowful
          Mysteries
+ The  5  Joyful Mysteries
+ The  5  Glorious Mysteries
+ The  4  Evangelists
+ The  3  Wise Men
+ The 40  Days of Lent
+ The  4  Sundays of Advent
+ The  3  Persons of the
          Trinity
─────────────────────────
= The  116 Things
```

Using the principles of numerology, we now add 1 + 1 + 6.

The answer is 8.

GOD REDUX

How are Catholics faring? What of those who went in search of new gods to replace the one they grew up with, or those who embraced the concept of a world where God had turned His back, was dead, or had never existed at all? Are they among the ones who read *Chicken Soup for the Soul*, *The Celestine Prophecy*, *A Course in Miracles* and *Conversations with God*? What are these barely practicing or fallen-away Catholics searching for, and what will they find in today's Church if they have been away from it for a while?

Merely attending a once-a-week ceremony or maintaining a Catholic cultural tradition is evidently not enough for them. They seem to be looking for a greater sense of spirituality, both in their everyday lives and in their religious practice. They might be surprised to find, however, that in hundreds of parishes around the country other Catholics are trying to achieve exactly that. These Catholics are choosing service work—in soup kitchens, homeless shelters, AIDS hospices, and countless other places—rather than extra leisure time. They are trying to bring about a transformation not only within other people's lives but within their own as well. These thoroughly contemporary Catholics are also looking again at many of the marvelous Church traditions that have been cast out over the past several decades like the proverbial babies with the Vatican II bathwater.

There will always be a human need to aim higher in life and to reach deeper within ourselves—to treat others with love and compassion, to develop more of our own potential, to make peace with the universe. So don't be surprised if someday on your way to an appointment, or after the kids have been dispatched to school, you find yourself sitting in the back pews of a church with just one or two others, looking far beyond the stained glass and remembering something you thought you had lost.

ABOUT THE AUTHORS

Mary Jane Frances Cavolina was born in 1954 and grew up in the Bayside section of Queens, New York, where she attended Sacred Heart School. A model student, Jane once received a prayer book for never turning her head during Mass. She attended St. Mary's Girls' High School, where she perfected her understanding of the concept of purgatory, and went on to receive a B.A. Honors degree from Hunter College. Jane is the coauthor, with her sister Ellen Cavolina, of *How to Really Watch The Godfather.* She lives in Lambertville, New Jersey.

Jeffrey Allen Joseph Stone was born in Providence, Rhode Island, in 1955 and grew up in Westbrook and Gorham, Maine. He was baptized at an Italian parish in Providence, despite the fact that an associate pastor contended that neither "Jeffrey" nor "Allen" was a saint's name. Among his coauthors, Jeff is the only "public"—a public school student who attended CCD classes at a Catholic school on Saturdays and was accused, along with his fellow CCDers, of messing up the parochial kids' desks. Jeff graduated magna cum laude from Brown University in 1977. Now living in New York City, he is a coauthor of *Treasures of the Aquarians* and *What Color Is Your Toothbrush?*

Maureen Anne Teresa Kelly was born in 1957 and was baptized at Most Precious Blood Church in Denver. Her first confession was said at St. Pius X Church in Dallas, and she received her First Holy Communion at Holy Ghost Church in Houston. In parochial school she won a glow-in-the-dark plastic Madonna for selling Holy Childhood Christmas Seals and was a member of the Junior Altar Rosary Society, an organization of young Catholic girls dedicated to straightening church pews and dusting kneelers. She went on to St. Agnes Academy in Houston and Randolph-Macon Woman's College in Lynchburg, Virginia. A coauthor of *Working in France,* she lives in Pittsburgh.

Richard Glen Michael Davis was born in 1953 and was baptized at St. Valentine's Church in Cicero, Illinois. After attending Sacred Heart, St. Elizabeth of Hungary, Mary Queen of Heaven, and Christ the King schools, he graduated from Montini High School—Montini being the surname of Pope Paul VI—and went on to receive a B.A. from the University of Illinois. Richard, who lives in Glendale, California, is a coauthor of *Treasures of the Aquarians* and *What Color Is Your Toothbrush?* He has written for the *Los Angeles Times* magazine, the *Los Angeles Times* and other publications.

PHOTO CREDITS

Grateful acknowledgment is made to the following:

Art Resource: pages 135, 138.   Andrea Kelly: page 68. N.Y. Daily News Photo: page 140.   Sotheby Parke-Bernet: page 143.   Jeff Stone: page 133.   Ken Robbins: pages 2, 39, 118, 123.   Wide World Photos: page 129.   Laura Worsham: pages 1, 36, 52, 101, 102, 103, 108, 119, 164, 165, 194.   AP/Wide World Photos: pages 151, 169, 173, 192, 210, 215.   Sister Catherine Grabowski, R.S.M., page 161.   The Bettmann Archive, pages 201, 202.